GOYA

Portrait of a Man, 1773–75

The Dog, 1820–23

Letter to the Vice-President of the Royal Academy

The Burial of the Sardine, 1812–19

18th-century etching tools

The Sleep of Reason, 1797–98

Asmodea, 1820–23

EYEWITNESS ◉ ART

GOYA

PATRICIA WRIGHT

I Am Still Learning, 1824–25

The Wedding, 1791–92

Self-Portrait,
1795–97

Tapestry bobbins

Allegory of
Wellington

DORLING KINDERSLEY
LONDON • NEW YORK • STUTTGART
IN ASSOCIATION WITH
THE NATIONAL GALLERY, LONDON

Letter to Zapater

Duel with Cudgels, 1820–23

And They are Wild Beasts,
c. 1812–15

A DORLING KINDERSLEY BOOK

For Sean

Editor Helen Castle
Art editor Liz Sephton
Assistant editor Louise Candlish
Assistant designer Simon Murrell
Senior editor Gwen Edmonds
Managing editor Sean Moore
Managing art editor Toni Kay
Picture researchers Julia Harris-Voss
and Jo Evans
DTP designer Zirrinia Austin
Production controller Meryl Silbert

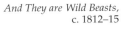

Plaque marking Goya's birthplace

This Eyewitness ®/™ Art book
first published in Great Britain in 1993 by
Dorling Kindersley Limited,
9 Henrietta Street, London WC2E 8PS

A CIP catalogue record for this book is
available from the British Library

ISBN 0 7513 1038 7

Colour reproduction by GRB Editrice s.r.l.
Printed in Italy by A. Mondadori Editore, Verona

Portrait of Goya,
Vincente López, 1828

Case for the Academician's
voting cabinet

Academician's
voting
cabinet

Goya's baptism record

*The Wounded
Mason*, 1786–87

Contents

The Milkmaid of Bordeaux, 1825–27

A modest beginning

GOYA'S POSITION TODAY as one of the world's greatest artists is all the more remarkable when we consider his inauspicious beginnings. He was born on the 30 March 1746, in Fuendetodos, a small rural village near Saragossa, in the Aragon region of northern Spain. As the son of a craftsman – a master gilder – Goya's earliest years were spent within the close confines of the village. Later, however, his family returned to their home town of Saragossa, where Goya spent four years at an *Escuelas Pías* – a school attached to a monastery. It was there that he met his lifelong friend and confidant, Martín Zapater (p. 10). By the time he was 13, Goya was apprenticed at the studio of Saragossa's master painter, José Luzán. Goya's first attempts to establish himself in Madrid and to acquire an academic training, however, met only with bitter disappointment. His modest background and lack of favourable connections worked against him. In 1770, at the age of 24, Goya departed for Italy, hoping to meet with more success at the academies there.

VIEW OF FUENDETODOS
The village of Goya's early childhood is built on an exposed hilltop, overlooking Aragon's harsh, windswept landscape.

This plaque on the outer wall of a house (below) in Fuendetodos marks Goya's birthplace.

GOYA'S HOUSE
Goya's family moved from Saragossa into his first home, in Fuendetodos, through financial necessity. The house belonged to his mother's once noble family. Goya's immediate family remained poor – the parish records of 1781 state that his father "made no will since he had nothing".

GOYA'S FIRST WORLD
This is the humble interior of Goya's birthplace. He was the third of five children, and the only one to attain financial success, although Carmilo, the youngest, became a priest.

GOYA'S BAPTISM RECORD
This register shows that Goya was baptised Francisco Joseph Goya, on 31 March 1746, only a day after his birth.

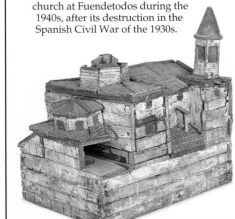

THE VIRGIN OF THE ASSUMPTION
Local children made this model of the church at Fuendetodos during the 1940s, after its destruction in the Spanish Civil War of the 1930s.

EARLIEST KNOWN WORK
Goya received his first commission to decorate a reliquary cabinet in the church at Fuendetodos, when he was about 16, and nearing the end of his apprenticeship. Unfortunately, it was destroyed along with the church (below left) in 1936.

FOLLOWING BAYEU TO MADRID
In 1763, the leading Aragonese artist Francisco Bayeu (1734–95) was called to Madrid by Anton Raphael Mengs (p. 11), First Painter to King Charles III. Shortly afterwards, Bayeu brought his younger brother Ramón, to Madrid establishing him at the Royal Academy. Goya's own applications to join the Academy that year, and three years later, were all rejected.

Madrid, as it would have appeared to Goya in 1763

COMPETING IN ROME
During 1770, Goya studied in both Rome and Parma, and learned the technique of fresco painting. In 1771, he was awarded second place in a competition at Parma's Academy of Fine Art, and received honourable mention for his entry, *Hannibal Crossing the Alps* – now lost.

THE ALLEGORY OF AGRICULTURE AND COMMERCE
Francisco Bayeu; c.1770; c. 24 x 15 cm (9½ x 6 in)
A successful painter at the Spanish court, Francisco Bayeu was an important role model for the young Goya. Only 12 years Goya's senior, Bayeu was also from Saragossa. While in Parma, Goya chose to refer to himself as a "pupil of Bayeu", rather than to associate with his true master, Luzán. Bayeu's style was a fusion of Meng's Neo-Classicism and Tiepolo's Italian Rococo (p. 63).

SELF-PORTRAIT
c.1771–75; 58 x 44 cm (22¾ x 17¼ in)
Here, Goya appears as a determined, almost belligerent, young man. In spite of his enormous talent, so evident in the strength of this early work, it was his determination that enabled him to transcend his humble background. Ramón Bayeu (1746–93), Francisco's younger brother, and Goya's contemporary, was a mediocre painter who imitated his successful brother's style, but, because of his brother's connections, succeeded first where Goya failed. Although the Bayeus were family acquaintances of Goya's, Goya did not enjoy the benefit of Francisco's influence until after 1773, when he married his sister (p. 8)

Success in Saragossa

W HEN GOYA RETURNED TO SPAIN from Italy, in 1771, he settled in Saragossa, the capital of Aragon, his native region. There, despite his lack of an academic training, he was awarded his first important commission: to produce six paintings for the Palace of Sobradiel, the official residence of the Counts of Gabardo. He also won a competition to paint frescoes (p. 63) for the Cathedral of El Pilar. In July 1773, when Goya was 27, he married Josefa Bayeu, the sister of Francisco and Ramón Bayeu. This marriage forged an important link between the painters, and though Goya's relationship with Francisco Bayeu proved to be stormy, soured by professional rivalry and by insecurity on Goya's part, it was of considerable value to his career. Goya remained in Saragossa for the first year of his marriage, where he executed an ambitious commission for the Monastery of Aula Dei. A remarkable achievement, it denoted the culmination of the first phase of his career, before he was summoned to Madrid as a result of his new family connection with the Bayeus.

THE CATHEDRAL OF EL PILAR
The Cathedral of Our Lady of the Pillar was the most magnificent church in Saragossa. It was also the scene of Goya's acrimonious split with Bayeu in 1781 (pp. 16–17).

DRAWING OF AN ANGEL'S HEAD
1772; 43.5 x 34 cm (17 x 13¼ in); red chalk on paper
The boldness of Goya's draughtsmanship can be readily seen in this powerful drawing. His angel portrays the worldly and very physical vitality of a robust young woman. She is one of several preparatory studies of angels that Goya produced for his *Adoration of the Name of God* fresco (below).

ADORATION OF THE NAME OF GOD
1772; 7 x 15 m (22¾ x 49¼ ft); fresco
Goya completed this large fresco for the *coreto*, or small choir, of the Cathedral of El Pilar in just four months. His technical facility and loose handling of paint, so characteristic of his later works, are evident here. However, the composition emulates the style of the Rococo genius Giambattista Tiepolo (1696–1770), who Goya had studied in Italy (pp. 6–7), and also echoes that of the court painter Corrado Giaquinto (1703–1765), whose work he would have seen in Madrid.

DISTANT TREES
The trees are painted as distinctly flat decoration – in complete contrast to the voluminous, larger-than-life, statuesque figures.

SIMPLIFIED FORM
The dramatically simplified forms in this early work, and almost total absence of surface detail, characterize Goya's late phase, and are especially evident in his last great fresco (pp. 32–33).

SUSPENDED MOVEMENT
All motion is suspended as the operation is performed on the baby. The wide figure shown from the back possesses remarkable still-ness and gravity, accentuated by the repeated use of verticals.

The Circumcision

1774; 3.1 x 5.2 m (10¼ x 17 ft); oil on plaster

This is a detail taken from *The Circumcision*, one of 11 large wall-paintings that Goya completed in the space of just a year for the chapel of the Carthusian monastery of Aula Dei, a few kilometres outside Saragossa. Goya's rejection of the classical tradition of smooth, evenly applied paint and uninterrupted surface is replaced with his "modern" and distinctly sketch-like, broad handling of paint – most noticeable in the statuesque forms of the figures.

CHAPEL OF AULA DEI
Painted directly with oils onto plaster walls (p. 54), Goya's paintings made up the entire decorative scheme for this chapel (right) in the Carthusian monastery.

THE VIRGIN OF THE PILLAR
1775–80; 78 x 52 cm (30½ x 20½ in)
The Virgin of the Pillar was one of the most popular religious subjects in Saragossa – her shrine attracted pilgrims from all over Europe. In 1641, an ecclesiastical trial had officially authenticated the miracle. This small painting by Goya was commissioned for domestic worship.

ENGRAVING OF THE VIRGIN OF THE PILLAR
This popular representation of Our Lady of the Pillar enthroned symbolizes the miraculous episode that had led to the cult in Saragossa. According to legend, a young beggar, Miguel Juan Pellicer, crippled by an accident in 1637, found his amputated leg restored after praying to the Virgin.

PORTRAIT OF A MAN
c.1773–75; 32 x 43 cm (12½ x 16¼ in)
This beautiful unfinished portrait is something of a mystery. It is possibly an early self-portrait by Goya, painted when he was still living in Saragossa, or even after his move to Madrid in 1774. Alternatively, it could be a portrait of an unknown man by Francisco Bayeu. The latter seems more likely, for Goya's other early self-portraits (p. 7) reveal a very different hair and skin colouring.

Goya at thirty

In 1774, Goya was called to Madrid by Mengs (right), the King's First Painter, to work at the Royal Tapestry Factory under Francisco Bayeu's direct supervision. He was employed there, on and off, for almost 20 years, producing cartoons – full-scale oil paintings that the weavers copied exactly into wool. Goya's earliest cartoons reveal two overriding material concerns: to satisfy Bayeu's expectations, and to maintain his own position. The Tapestry Factory was his only access to Court circles, and Goya was certainly ambitious. In Saragossa, at 28, he was already in the top tax bracket, earning more than his former master, Luzán. In fact, throughout his life he showed an intense desire for financial security; perhaps a legacy of his humble origins. Goya's powerful artistic personality, however, soon became apparent in his cartoons, which were injected with his own personal vision of contemporary Spanish life and modern customs (p. 11).

The Hunter and his Dogs

1775; 262 x 71 cm (103 x 27¾ in)
The distinctive character of Goya's earlier works (pp. 8–9) is not readily apparent in his first cartoons, such as this, which reveals Francisco Bayeu's influence in its strong, dense colours, and rather stolid handling of paint. This cartoon's contrived appearance is also due to its vertical format. It was the design for a *rinconeras*, a tapestry that filled corner spaces.

LETTER TO ZAPATER
This is one of 122 surviving letters from Goya to his lifelong friend Martín Zapater (p. 28). The coded "messages" and drawings are typical. Hunting was one of Goya's favourite topics.

DOGS IN LEASH
1775; 112 x 170 cm (44 x 66¼ in)
Goya's first series of cartoons for the Royal Family's autumn residence, the Escorial Palace, reflected King Charles III's interests. There was one fishing, and eight hunting scenes. Unlike his successor, the King led a life of strict routine, which revolved solely around the Church, politics, his family, and a passion for hunting.

18TH-CENTURY RIFLE
Goya shared King Charles III's love of hunting. He was, as he states in his letters to Zapater, a very successful huntsman. In later years, Goya painted a portrait of the visibly frail king, in hunting dress, with rifle and gun dog.

MINIATURE SELF-PORTRAIT
Anton Mengs;
6.5 x 5.5 cm (2½ x 2 in)
The Dresden-born, Neo-Classical painter Mengs (1728–79) studied art from a young age in Rome. His art reflected the renewed interest in the classical, revived by excavations such as Pompeii.

CHARLES III
Anton Mengs;
1761; 154 x 110 cm (60½ x 43¼ in)
In 1762, Charles III appointed Mengs First Painter to the King. This portrait was his favourite, doubtless for its plain treatment of his odd physiognomy.

SPANISH PASTIMES
This popular 18th-century engraving is similar to Goya's depiction of Spanish pastimes. Goya preferred to paint "real" Spanish types, rather than the previously fashionable French scenes.

NEW TASTES AT COURT
In 1776, the future Charles IV, the Prince of Asturias, and his wife, María Luisa of Parma, had been married 11 years (right). It is likely that María Luisa, known for her extravagant tastes and interest in art, chose the subjects of the second series of cartoons for the Royal Palace, the Pardo. Schematically, they were far more sophisticated than Goya's earlier hunting scenes.

DRAWING FOR THE PICNIC
1776; 20 x 28 cm (7¾ x 11 in); black chalk and heightened white, on blue paper
This sketch for *The Picnic* shows a young urban *majo* (pp. 36–37), or city dweller, smoking a cigar and sporting a colourful *redecilla* (hairnet). Through this image of the nonchalant young man and his rowdy companions, Goya provides us with a vivid scene of popular culture in 18th-century Madrid.

The Picnic
1776; 272 x 295 (107 x 116 in)
Goya's ability to assimilate styles and to adapt to working methods meant that he was soon allowed greater artistic freedom at the Tapestry Factory. *The Picnic* is a departure from the traditional themes he was encouraged to paint under Bayeu. In his invoice of 1776, Goya described *The Picnic* as: "a painting that I, Francisco Goya have executed (of my own Invention)". By this statement of authorship, Goya ensured he receive the maximum payment for his work, since only a third of the sum would be paid for a cartoon done after another artist's design.

The Royal Tapestry Factory

G OYA'S TAPESTRY CARTOONS were not originally awarded the importance that they are today; they were regarded as a means to an end – as Francisco Bayeu complained in 1786, "no painter of the first class, or of recognized merit, would want to paint works that don't serve to his credit, and end up in the factory without the public seeing them". Aside from being decorative, woollen tapestries insulated the palaces from the cold, covering the walls of spacious rooms – including the areas above doors (*sobrepuertas*, p. 14), and above and between windows (*sobrebalcones* and *rinconeras*, p. 10).

A spinning wheel from the Tapestry Factory

THE AMATEUR BULLFIGHT
1780; 259 x 136 cm (101¼ x 53½ in)
The figure in red is thought to be a self-portrait.

The Crockery Vendor

1779; 259 x 220 cm (101¼ x 86½ in)
Sixty-three of Goya's tapestry designs are known today (some only through their tapestries). This cartoon, with its theme of selling and displaying – on various social levels – is interesting as a casual "incidental" scene, but also as one which uses multiple focal points.

THE FINISHED TAPESTRY
Maintaining the tapestries in good condition was an important part of a palace's housekeeping. Works such as *The Swing*, after a cartoon by Goya, were regularly washed in the river to prevent them from being eaten by moths.

TAPESTRY BOBBINS
These slender wooden bobbins, are still in use today at the Royal Tapestry Factory. They are designed with pointed tips, which are well suited to the delicate, painstaking weaving process (right).

Original loom from the Royal Tapestry Factory

A great many shades of colour are required by the weavers

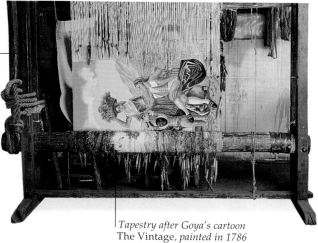

TAPESTRY WEAVER
Weavers worked the tapestries from the back, studying the cartoon through the threads on the loom. This process, as shown, is still practised today at the Royal Tapestry Factory of Santa Bárbara, Madrid. This factory was founded by Francisco Vandergoten to produce tapestries for the royal palaces. He was the son of the Flemish tapestry manufacturer Jacob Vandergoten, who first came to Madrid in 1720 to teach his weaving skills to the Spanish.

Tapestry after Goya's cartoon The Vintage, *painted in 1786*

THE WASHERWOMEN
c.1776–78; 86.5 x 59 cm (34 x 23 in); oil sketch
Initial sketches for cartoons, such as this (above), remained the artists' property, but the finished cartoons (below right) were rolled and stored away once the tapestries were completed. Goya's cartoons were not discovered until the late 19th century, in the basement of the Royal Palace in Madrid.

The Washerwomen

1780; 218 x 166 cm (85¼ x 65¼ in)
This cartoon reveals Goya's growing interest in landscape, which he described in detail in his account of the painting as "a gay sky, a lot of trees on the side of the river, parts of which can be seen winding towards thickets and snowy mountains in the distance". Its light-hearted, frivolous mood particularly reflects the taste of the Prince and Princess of Asturias.

Tradition and invention

Colour swatches

Lead white　Naples yellow　Yellow ochre

Light red

Vermilion

Prussian blue

Terre verte

Ivory black

COLOURED GROUNDS
Like Velázquez
(pp. 16–17), Goya used
coloured grounds, which
included yellow, orange,
and red, applied over a
white lead primer (p. 63).
A light ground, such as
a yellow, contributed to
a painting's luminosity.

The Parasol

1777; 104 x 152 cm (40¾ x 59¾ in)

This cartoon was designed for a *sobrepuerta* – a tapestry
positioned above a doorway. By using the simple device of
positioning the two figures on the highest point of a hill and
silhouetting them against the sky, Goya created a convincing
sensation of height, in keeping with the tapestry's high location.
The young woman's docile lap-dog symbolizes the role of her
attentive companion. Her prominently displayed closed fan,
and coquettish expression, indicate who has the upper hand.

THE FRESH VITALITY AND NATURALISM of Goya's work
greatly appealed to the Prince and Princess of Asturias
(p. 11), who were enthusiastic patrons of Spanish art.
In 1777, Goya produced four cartoons for the Prince's
dining hall in the Pardo Palace – the Royal Family's
winter residence outside Madrid. Among these was
one of his finest, *The Parasol*. Its subtle half-tones,
brilliant colour, and unorthodox dynamic composition
undermined the purely decorative conventions of
the tapestry cartoon. Hung in its intended setting,
as a tapestry, *The Parasol's* self-conscious,
dainty elegance and opulence would have
been offset by *The Toper*, a companion
piece of rough simplicity, depicting two
rural youths eating bread and radishes.
In this pairing, Goya's love of opposites
and counterbalance first becomes apparent,
prefiguring his later tendency to visualize
themes in series of related works.

A touch of white was applied to enliven the eyes in shadow

Each leaf is made up of one bold brushstroke

FACE TO FACE

There is a surprisingly confrontational element to *The Parasol* – the figures are brought right up to the picture plane (p. 63). Instead of showing us a distant image of picturesque intimacy, Goya suggests a dialogue between the alert young woman and her audience, the viewer. He has also recreated the low light of a late afternoon, which catches on the lower side of forms and emphasizes the elevation of the figures. The beautiful pool of light around the woman's left eye is reflected off the underside of the parasol (which acts as a kind of bowl of trapped light) and gently illuminates the rest of her face, while shading it from direct sunlight. Her lips are almost without definition, giving the woman's playful expression an extra mobility.

CONFIDENT BRUSHWORK

This weak-looking sapling in the right of the picture is a useful compositional device, which helps to balance the heavy solidity of the wall. The leaves are painted with great confidence, almost nonchalance, one stroke per leaf – each revealing Goya's particular gesture and character of brushwork – over a sky that he had allowed to dry first.

The trees graduate in colour from dark to light

HANDLING OF THE PAINT

At this point in his career, Goya applied paint in the traditional manner – evenly, opaquely, and in thick strokes – concealing the coloured ground. This method contrasts greatly with that of Goya's later works, in which the paint is remarkably liquid and transparent.

DISTANCE AND COLOUR

Goya renounced the mellow atmospherics of his predecessors and contemporaries in favour of a raw and brilliant light. This was the effect of his use of light-coloured grounds (p. 14, top). He also boldly applied distinct bands of colour and tone to give a sense of recession. It is the fresh rawness of these colours that leaves the modern viewer with the impression that the painting has been newly cleaned.

A new direction

CHRIST ON THE CROSS
Diego Velázquez; c.1631; 100 x 57 cm (39¼ x 22¼ in)
The pride of the royal collections were undoubtedly the works of the great Spanish master Diego Velázquez (1599–1660) – Painter to King Philip IV of Spain for almost 40 years. The dark void of Goya's crucifixion (below) reveals his debt to Velázquez.

By 1780, SPAIN WAS AT WAR with England, and Goya's work at the Tapestry Factory was suspended. Through Francisco Bayeu's support, Goya at last gained membership to the Royal Academy in Madrid. His established contacts with the royal household allowed him access to the magnificent royal collections, and, leading up to the war, Goya produced a series of prints after paintings by Velázquez – his earliest forays into print-making. During this time, he also produced his first important etching, *The Garotted Man*. At the end of the year, Goya left Madrid to collaborate with Francisco Bayeu, in their home town of Saragossa. It was a move that proved disastrous, provoking a violent rift in their relationship. Goya returned to Madrid in 1781, humiliated. However, he soon received an important royal commission for an altarpiece in the new church of San Francisco el Grande, in which he proudly included his own self-portrait (far right).

CHRIST ON THE CROSS
1780; 255 x 153 cm (100½ x 60¼ in)
This crucifixion scene, which was submitted by Goya to the Royal Academy, reveals his shrewd, business instincts, and the lengths to which he was prepared to go in order to secure his future. It effectively combined the achievements of Spain's greatest painter, Velázquez, with the acclaimed style of Goya's most distinguished contemporary, Anton Mengs (p. 11). Through this assimilation of styles, Goya hoped to win the approval of the Academicians, and attract the interest of potential patrons. However, Goya's crucifixion does not compare well with its model, Velázquez' great work (top left). There is something distasteful in the contrast between Velázquez' portrayal of Christ as an object of contemplation and devotion, and Goya's dramatic creation, which, though beautifully painted, was executed as a showpiece.

CHRIST ON THE CROSS
Anton Mengs; 1761–69; 198 x 115 cm (77⅞ x 45¼ in)
Goya made direct reference to Mengs' highly acclaimed crucifixion (right), adopting the same rhythms and twists in the body of Christ. However, he departed from Mengs' overtly classical approach to physical suffering, in which Christ appears transcendentally serene. Instead, Goya chose to channel all the emotive power and human significance of Jesus' death into the single focal point of Christ's upturned face.

THE GAROTTED MAN
1778–80; 33 x 21.5 cm
(13 x 8½ in); etching
In its graphic clarity and emotional impact, Goya's first known, original etching resembles that of his later prints.

Hand-held, 18th-century etching tools

A FRAGILE SURFACE
Goya's original etched copper-plates were steel-plated in the 19th century to protect their surface.

SEBASTIAN DE MORRA
1778; 21.5 x 15 cm
(8½ x 6 in); etching
Goya had copied engravings after master paintings at Luzán's studio in Saragossa. His first prints were also copies – such as this etching after Velázquez' portrait of de Morra (c.1644). Goya's copies reveal, above all, his own independent expression. As published copies, they were not a success, as his own authorship was too apparent.

Sacada, y granada, del Quadro original, de D. Diego Velazquez, en que representa, al vivo vn Enano del S. Phelipe IV, por D. Francisco Goya Pintor. Existe en el R.l Palacio de Madrid. Año de 1778.

THE QUEEN OF THE MARTYRS
1780–81; cupola fresco
In 1780, Goya was commissioned to decorate one of the domes of the Cathedral of El Pilar in Saragossa. His brother-in-law, Francisco Bayeu, was originally awarded the scheme, but recruited Goya, and Ramón Bayeu, to continue the work under his supervision. When Goya was forced to re-paint this fresco, because of its unfinished appearance, the tension and rivalry that had been building up for years, erupted, causing a rift in their relation-ship. It was not healed until six years later (pp. 18–19). Goya could not accept such humiliation, and returned to Madrid. He declared to Zapater his disgust for "those vile men who had so little faith in my merit".

ST. BERNARDINE OF SIENA
1782–83; 480 x 300 cm (188¾ x 118 in)
The commission to paint one of the seven altar panels for the new church of San Francisco el Grande in Madrid gave Goya's talent full rein – unhampered by Francisco Bayeu's interference. Since Bayeu was one of six other distinguished Academicians invited to paint an altarpiece, Goya realised that his reputation was at stake. In contrast to the speedy execution of his earlier religious frescoes, he spent two years on this painting. It was a public success, he had created a lively sense of depth and space within a restricted and difficult format.

Fashionable portrait painter

IT IS UNLIKELY GOYA WOULD HAVE ATTAINED great status or financial reward had he continued to paint only religious works and tapestry cartoons. At this relatively early stage in his career, his most pressing concern was to secure patrons (particularly in light of the disastrous "Saragossa affair" [p. 17], when he lost Francisco Bayeu's support). Goya's election to the Royal Academy in 1780 (p. 16) brought him his first important portrait commissions. By 1783, he believed that he had found a long-term patron and "protector" in the Infante Don Luis, the disgraced brother of Charles III. This arrangement, however, was to be short-lived, ending with the Infante's death in 1785.

A few months later, Goya's fortune turned again, when he was elected Deputy Director of Painting at the Academy – a prestigious position that generated lucrative portrait commissions. In 1786, his appointment as Painter to the King assured him the financial security of a regular salary.

SELF-PORTRAIT AT EASEL
c. 1790–95; 42 x 28 cm (16½ x 11 in)
This self-portrait qualifies Goya's statement: "I had three masters, Rembrandt, Velázquez, and Nature". Its small scale, and use of light conjure up *An Artist in the Studio*, by Rembrandt (1606–69), which employs equally dramatic *chiaroscuro* (p. 64). Here, Goya's hat is fitted with candles to enable him to paint in a low light.

THE COUNT OF FLORIDABLANCA AND GOYA
1783; 262 x 166 cm (103¼ x 65¼ in)
This elaborate and rather contrived portrait of the First Secretary of State, Count Floridablanca, was Goya's first important commission. Goya included himself – as a low ranking public servant, shown from the back, and diminished in scale. The Count, however, did not like the painting and only paid Goya reluctantly.

THE FAMILY OF THE INFANTE DON LUIS
1784; 248 x 330 cm (97½ x 129¼ in)
A year after his very formal portrait of Count Floridablanca, Goya painted the extraordinarily informal *Family of the Infante Don Luis*. Although again shown from the back, Goya is now in full command of the situation. Conventional hierarchy is ignored here, and different social classes mix. The structure of the composition was appropriately unorthodox, since Don Luis was guilty of marrying beneath his class. Goya's brilliant play of light compensates for the painting's lack of a single focus, which similarly subverts pictorial convention.

CARNATION

The carnation was a symbolic feature of 15th and 16th-century Flemish portraiture. A pink carnation, as in Mengs' portrait (right), denotes betrothal and love, but it can also be used to signify motherhood.

MARIA LUISA OF PARMA
Anton Mengs; 1756; 48 x 38 cm (18¾ x 14¼ in)
Mengs' greatest achievements were his portraits, such as this beautiful painting of the future Queen (p. 11). His blend of Neo-Classical objectivity (p. 63), and sensitivity to colour and form, created works of powerful intensity. They were important role models for Goya's early portraits.

PORCELAIN COMPLEXION
Goya created his delicate flesh tints through a mixture of light red and terre verte (green), moderated with white (pp. 14–15). He applied touches of full-strength vermilion (red) to enliven colour on lips and and cheeks.

WET-IN-WET
Goya's working practice, like Velázquez', was to cover the canvas in one session, adding detail later. This first-stage technique of "wet-in-wet" resulted in a *sfumato* appearance – a softness of definition, created by the colours and tones overlapping and blending into each other.

WOMEN IN LANDSCAPES
Goya's and Mengs' portraits both follow the French and English tradition of painting women against idealized landscape "backdrops" – considered suitable settings with which to display their feminine qualities and family status.

The Marchioness of Pontejos

c. 1786; 211 x 126 cm (83 x 49½ in)
The most prestigious portraits were full length, as they were expensive to commission. This extraordinary Rococo portrait of the Marchioness of Pontejos, resembling a porcelain figurine, was probably commissioned to celebrate her marriage to the brother of Count Floridablanca (left). Unlike the French and English, the Spanish were prepared to pose at length, which helps to explain this painting's stiff, expressionless quality.

Cartoons for two kings

CHARLES III
c.1786–88; 206 x 130 cm
(81 x 51 in)
Charles III preferred
Mengs' (p. 11) sober,
pragmatic portraits
to those by Goya.

**MINIATURE OF
CHARLES III**
As the so-called
"reformers' king",
Charles III improved
living conditions in
Madrid with practical
advances such as
sewage systems and
new roads.

IN 1786, AFTER A BREAK OF SIX YEARS, Goya returned to
work at the Royal Tapestry Factory. Now a successful
portrait painter, he was reluctant to concentrate again on
tapestry cartoons; but as a newly appointed Painter to King
Charles III, it constituted a duty. However, with the death of
Charles III, two years later, Spanish art entered a new phase
under Charles IV and María Luisa. The prevailing fashion
at Court for all things French and Italian gave way to a new
apppreciation of Spanish life and customs. Goya was soon
promoted to the exalted position of First Painter to the King:
an appointment that had been dominated for many years by
foreign artists such as Anton Mengs (p. 11).
He painted a new series of six cartoons for
the dining-room of the Pardo Palace, which depicted
the four seasons and two "social" scenes; and started
on a second scheme for the Princesses' bedchamber.

**THE WOUNDED
MASON**
1786–87; 268 x 110 cm
(105½ x 43¼ in)
The sketch for this
cartoon reveals Goya's
original irreverent
subject of the drunken
mason, which he
transformed into this
solemn work by simply
altering the facial
expressions of the
mason's work-mates.
What was originally a
humourous "cameo" of
working life, depicting
the drunken mason
being transported
home, now became
this tender image of
solicitation. The
original sketch was
rejected, since it was
intended for the king's
dining-room, and was
perhaps deemed in
poor taste. Possibly,
it reflected some
of the Court's
habits too closely.

WINTER
1786–87; 275 x 293 cm (108¼ x 115¼ in)
Here, peasants are depicted returning home with a freshly killed pig
during a year of famine. Goya treated this popular pastoral subject
with a stark, new realism. Rather than representing man in harmony
with nature, he revealed a cruel, harsh existence – a struggle for
survival against the blind indifference of the elements.

SUMMER
1786; 34 x 76 cm
(13¼ x 29¾ in); oil sketch
This is the sketch for the
largest tapestry cartoon
that Goya ever made,
which is over 6.40 m
(21 feet) wide. All
sketches had to receive
royal approval, before
work could begin on
the full-scale cartoons.

PORTRAIT OF CHARLES IV
1789; 126 x 94 cm (49½ x 37)
Goya painted this portrait in 1789, when King Charles IV ascended the throne. In the same momentous year, Goya was appointed First Court Painter, and the French Revolution broke out, which was to have long-term consequences for the Spanish Royal Family (pp. 38–39). Unlike his father, Charles IV was a weak man, who having married young, was dominated by his wife. He did, however, share his father's passion for hunting.

THE STRAW MANIKIN
1791–92; 267 x 160 cm
(105 x 62¾ in)
As Painter to King Charles III, and First Court Painter to Charles IV, Goya received a regular salary, whereas previously, he had been paid separately for each tapestry cartoon. Eager to detach himself from his commitments at the Royal Tapestry Factory, Goya only continued to produce cartoons under the threat of having his salary suspended. *The Straw Manikin* was one of the last cartoons he painted. Its uncomfortable mixture of humour and sinister sub-narrative moves a step closer to Goya's masterful articulation of the language of satire (pp. 28-29).

THE WEDDING
1791–92; 267 x 293 cm (105 x 115¼ in)
Goya's sharp sense of humour is evident in this image of opposites – a pretty young woman is marrying a hideous older man, to the barely disguised amusement of their wedding guests. The imbalance is heightened by the pairing of a young child, precariously balancing on a cart, to the left, with an old man on unsteady legs, to the right. The wedding party, led Pied Piper-style through the streets, is at the centre of the design, mediating between the equal, but opposing, conditions of childhood and extreme old age that are free from the considerations governing middle life.

THE MEADOW OF ST. ISIDORE *(below)*
1788; 44 x 94 cm (17¼ x 37in); oil sketch
This brilliant panoramic landscape of a crowded meadow, overlooking the distant city of Madrid, is one of five preparatory sketches for a cartoon, intended for the Princesses ' bedchamber in the Pardo. The outlined figures in the foreground present a happy image of relaxed decadence – drinking and resting under parasols. Such a mass of detail and subtle treatment of space proved too complicated a problem for the tapestry weavers. The happy atmosphere of the meadow has a sinister twin in Goya's later Black Painting, *The Pilgrimage of St. Isidore* – created within a similarly wide format (pp. 54–55).

CONVENT OF ST. ISIDORE
This convent was dedicated to Saint Isidore, the patron saint of Madrid. Goya's painting (below) shows the 15 May festivities, in honour of the saint.

Goya and the child

GOYA IS MOST OFTEN remembered for his Black Paintings (pp. 48-55), but, for all the horror and grotesque imagery running through his work, he produced a great many paintings of unadulterated beauty. Goya reserved a special affection for children, and his portrayal of them remained consistently tender. When his son, Javier, was born on 2 December 1784, Goya and his wife, Josefa (p.8) had already been married for 11 years. Javier was their first, and only, child to survive infancy. Goya's love for his son is well documented. In 1788 he proudly wrote (p. 28): "I have a son of four years, who is so beautiful people look at him in the streets of Madrid." During the same year, Goya painted one of his most exquisite works, his portrait of Manuel Osorio de Zuñiga, a boy of almost exactly the same age as Javier.

CHILDISH RAGE
c.1824-8; black chalk
Goya made this drawing towards the end of his life, when he produced many images of childhood and of old age. The economy of line here, is truly exceptional – the succinct expression of childish rage all the more powerful for its simplicity.

BUT HE BROKE THE PITCHER
1797–98; 20.5 x 15 cm (8 x 5¾ in); etching and aquatint
This technically brilliant work belongs to Goya's *Caprices* series (pp. 28–29). What seems at first a humourous domestic image, soon becomes alarming. The powerlessness and vulnerability of the child are off-set against the woman's savage expression, as she is reduced to clawing and biting at his clothes.

BOYS PLAYING AT SOLDIERS
c.1777–85; 29 x 42 cm (11¼ x 16½ in)
One of six paintings of children playing, this was probably a preparatory sketch for an incomplete series of cartoons. Goya often included children in his tapestries as figures of fun, in contrast to his more cynical themes of old age or the loss of innocence.

BOYS WITH MASTIFFS
1786–87; 112 x 145 cm (44 x 57 in)
A relatively early tapestry cartoon, this painting was designed for the dining-room in the Pardo Palace. It was executed with supreme confidence and great skill. The laces on the boy's waistcoat for instance, were painted in a single attempt. The solid, sculptural quality of *Boys with Mastiffs* is created through Goya's combination of a beautifully simple, luminous colour range of orange, red, blue and yellow, set against the solid neutral grey-browns of the earth and the dogs. This results in a simultaneous expression of colour and form. Goya's command of volume, weight, and tension between the boys and animals is remarkable.

THE LITTLE GIANTS
1791–92; 137 x 104 cm (53¾ x 40¾ in)
Goya returned to the theme of the giant many times; it became for him, a symbol of violence, ignorance and cruelty (pp. 39, 51 & 56). As such, it is difficult to look upon this children's game without finding subtle references in it to innocence betrayed.

Don Manuel Osorio de Manrique Zuñiga

c.1788; 127 x 101 cm (50 x 39¾ in)
This portrait of Manuel Osorio de Zuñiga, the four-year-old son of the Count and Countess of Altimara, was one of several by Goya of the Altimara family, commissioned for the Bank of Spain. Goya used the richness of the boy's clothes to highlight his pale delicacy. It was through a series of such contrasts that Goya created an overriding sense of the child's vulnerability.

A GENTLE CHILD
Children's latent cruelty was a common subject for contemporary satire. The English artist William Hogarth (1697–1764), for instance, showed just how cruel children could be to animals. Reversing that convention here, Goya presents Manuel as gentle and guileless, in a gloomy predatory setting.

THREE CATS
In 18th-century Spain, cats were symbolic of evil, and associated with witchcraft and sorcery. Their inclusion here is an allegory on the loss of innocence: the three large cats stare intensely at the uncaged bird, clearly waiting for their chance to pounce.

VISITING CARD
Goya made a formal record of Manuel Osorio de Zuñiga's name and date of birth along the bottom of the canvas. He incorporated his own signature, however, above it within the actual space of the painting – on an artist's card, which is held in the magpie's beak.

EMPTY SPACE
As was often the case with Goya's portraits of young children, there is no suggestion of an intimate space or background. The boy stands isolated in the midst of a featureless area, darkened by deep brown shadows. The inclusion of Manuel's clothes and toys at the bottom of the painting, give an indication of his social status and identity.

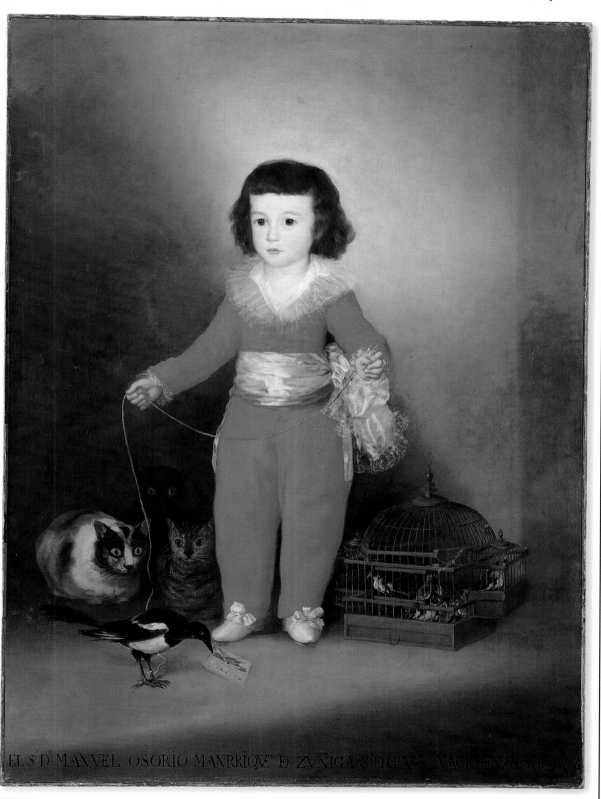

ELS^r Dⁿ MANVEL OSORIO MANRRIQVE D ZVÑIGA Sr DGINS NACIO EN ^s ANO. 84

Illness: a turning point

IN DECEMBER 1792, Goya was overcome by a devastating illness during a stay in Cadiz, where, he had been commissioned to paint a magnificent portrait of Sebastián Martínez (below, right) – a wealthy merchant and art collector. Unable to travel home, Goya remained at Martínez' house, and slowly recovered. During his stay, Goya began a series of small Cabinet Pictures, which mark the first free expression of his violent, and fantastical imagination. The illness left Goya totally deaf, and the trauma of sudden and noisy isolation from the world had a cathartic effect on his work – releasing the latent dark imagery, fully realized in his Black Paintings (pp. 48–51). Reluctant to return to the now onerous production of tapestry cartoons in Madrid, Goya prolonged his convalescence.

BUST OF GOYA
Despite his robust recovery from illness, Goya remained totally deaf for the rest of his life, and endured the clamorous noise of tinnitus.

PRISON SCENE
Goya was influenced by the *Carceri* (prison) series of etchings by the Italian architect Giovanni Piranesi (1720–78), in Martínez' extensive art collection.

DON SEBASTIAN MARTINEZ Y PEREZ
1792; 93 x 67.5 cm (36½ x 26½ in)
This is one of Goya's greatest portraits. The characterization of Martínez' proud, sensuous face epitomizes the painting's brilliance – remarkable for its unorthodox close-up positioning of the subject, and the beautiful simplicity of its colours.

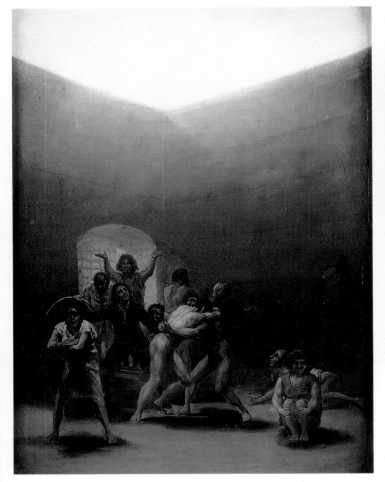

MADHOUSE AT SARAGOSSA
1794; 43.5 x 32.5 cm (17 x 12¾ in); oil on tin
"It is a scene I witnessed in Saragossa." Goya described his Cabinet Pictures as "observations for which there is normally no opportunity in commissioned works, which give no scope for fantasy or imagination". He wrote of this small, but disturbing work that it was a "madhouse scene, with two men fighting naked [including] the one who takes care of them by beating them up".

THE SHIPWRECK
1793–94; 50 x 32 cm (19½ x 12½ in); oil on tin

The Cabinet Pictures are characterized by their horrific subjects. This painting depicts the tragedy of a natural disaster, although the majority of the series concentrate on human nature's infinite capacity for cruelty (right). Goya sent these paintings to the Vice-President of the Royal Academy (below right), to be shown to the other professors.

PORTRAIT OF FRANCISCO BAYEU
1795; 112 x 84 cm (44 x 33 in)

Commissioned to paint this portrait after Bayeu's death on 4 August 1795, Goya copied it from one of Bayeu's own earlier self-portraits. This may account for a certain woodenness, most noticeable in the right arm. It is a powerful portrait nonetheless, with its disdainful, restless expression and beautiful silver-grey colour harmony.

BRIGANDS ATTACKING A COACH
1793–94; 50 x 32 cm (19½ x 12½ in); oil on tin

The delicate surface and small scale "cameo" quality of the Cabinet Pictures serves to make their content all the more horrific. This painting at first glance could be of a roadside picnic, or, at worst, a broken carriage-wheel; only on closer examination does the scene of cold-blooded murder become apparent. Goya's use of a tin support with a shiny surface facilitated fine brushwork – creating an enamelled effect.

LETTER TO BERNARDO DE IRIARTE
Goya sent this to Iriarte, Vice-President of the Royal Academy, with his Cabinet Pictures, to ask that he help him to sell them to compensate for the financial losses of his illness.

ACADEMICIANS' VOTING CABINET
On Bayeu's death (left), Goya was elected Director of Painting at the Royal Academy in Madrid. This strange object was the ballot box used by Academicians for electing candidates. Each member locked his vote in one of the tiny drawers around its perimeter.

25

"Only Goya"

GOYA'S RELATIONSHIP WITH the Duchess of Alba (right) has been the subject of much debate. Goya was clearly infatuated with her, but it is not certain whether they were lovers. They first met in 1795, when Goya was commissioned to paint the first of two full-length portraits of her. The following year, the Duchess' husband (below right), died suddenly at the age of 40. Goya was then in Andalusia, where the young widow retreated for her period of mourning, and he spent the summer with her on her estate. Either Goya's attentions were not returned, or the Duchess tired of the relationship fairly quickly. The bitterness that Goya consequently felt overflowed into his work. He kept her portrait (far right) until 1812 – which suggests it was an uncommissioned work – when he passed it on to his son Javier.

SELF-PORTRAIT
c.1795–97; 23.5 x 14.5 cm (9¼ x 5¾ in); Indian ink
Somewhat angst-ridden, Goya's portrayal of himself is also extremely romantic, hinting at his defiance and vitality, which was possibly a result of his relationship with the Duchess (right).

MARCHIONESS OF LA SOLANA
c. 1794–95; 183 x 124 cm (72 x 48¾ in)
The Marchioness was a confidante of the Duchess. She commissioned this portrait when she was dying, aged only 28. Goya's subtle, perceptive portrayal of the Marchioness sharply contrasts with his theatrical portraits of the Duchess.

THE DUCHESS AND HER DUENNA
1795; 31 x 25 cm (12¼ x 9¾ in)
This disturbing picture of the Duchess with her chaperone reveals a certain confusion on Goya's part, as he depicts her as being both sexually attractive and threatening.

THE DUCHESS OF ALBA HOLDING MARIA DE LA LUZ
1796–97; 10.5 x 9 cm (4¼ x 3½ in); indian ink wash
This affectionate sketch of the Duchess cradling a child belongs to Goya's first series of private drawings – out of which grew his great *Caprices* prints (pp. 28–29).

DUKE OF ALBA
1795; 195 x 126 (76¾ x 49½ in)
Ironically, Goya first met the Duchess of Alba through her husband, the Duke, who commissioned Goya's first two portraits of her.

This contemporary engraving is of the Andalusian bullfighter, Pedro Romero, and his trophy.

PEDRO ROMERO
c. 1795–98; 84 x 65 cm (33 x 25½ in)
The Duchesses Alba and Osuna were rivals, who each championed opposing matadors. Goya painted this stunning portrait of Romero, who was the protégé of the Duchess of Osuna.

HAUGHTY ARISTOCRAT
The Duchess of Alba was also rumoured to be the lover of Godoy, the Queen's favourite (p. 34). Her aristocratic standing and beauty made her Spain's first lady after the Queen.

PAINTED LADY
Goya wrote to Zapater that the Duchess came to his studio, "so that I could paint her face for her; I certainly find it more agreeable than painting canvas".

HIDDEN INSCRIPTION
"Only Goya" could be interpreted in two ways: either as a proclamation of the Duchess' love for Goya, or as Goya's own declaration of his genius.

The Duchess of Alba

1797; 210 x 149.5 cm (82½ x 58¾ in)
The cleaning of Goya's portrait of the Duchess of Alba revealed the words "Solo Goya" (Only Goya), which Goya himself had painted over at a later date. These enigmatic words – together with her two rings, worn side by side, and bearing the names Alba and Goya – are the basis of the belief that the two were involved in a love affair.

COMMEMORATIVE MONUMENT
1800–08; pen and indian ink on grey paper
Traditionally, this monument is supposed to have been designed by Goya for the Duchess, after her death in 1802. It is probable, however, that its association with the Duchess grew out of the mythology surrounding their relationship.

Caprice

THE NAME *CAPRICES* (*caprichos*) was used by Goya to describe his series of eighty satirical prints, produced between 1797 and 1799. They were Goya's first decisive political statement. Their overt social and political commentary, when compared to his earlier comic approach to drawing, suggests that Goya may have been influenced by his liberal friend, the dramatist Leandro Fernandéz Moratín (far right). When Moratín returned from a tour of Europe, he brought with him extensive notes about the caricatures he had seen in England, and their power to undermine the Establishment. In Spain, however, the Inquisition suppressed the public sale of *The Caprices* within 15 days, by ordering the withdrawal of all copies. The series format, which Goya adopted in the *Caprices* portfolio and repeated in his *Disasters of War* (pp. 40–41), *Proverbs* (pp. 52–53), and *Art of Bullfighting* (pp. 58–59), provided a perfect vehicle for his ceaselessly fertile imagination, and extraordinary graphic skills. By his death in 1828, he had fully exploited the medium's potential for expression and propaganda.

SELF-PORTRAIT WITH SPECTACLES
c.1797–1800; 63 x 49 cm (24¼ x 19¼ in)
Goya intended: "to banish harmful common beliefs and to perpetuate with this work of *caprices* the sound testimony of truth." The series was begun during a year of liberal rule, promoted by the Minister of Justice, Gaspar Jovellanos (p. 32).

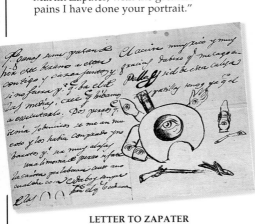

MARTIN ZAPATER Y CLAVERIA
1797; 83 x 64 cm (32½ x 25 in)
Goya's letters to his old school friend, the Saragossa merchant Martín Zapater, provide us with an important access to his private world. They remained close friends until Zapater's death in 1800. Goya dedicated this painting (above): "To my friend Martín Zapater, with the greatest pains I have done your portrait."

LETTER TO ZAPATER
The affectionate, bantering tone and rambling content of most of Goya's letters to Zapater would disappoint those searching for a key to Goya's ideas on art. This strange doodle, in his letter of 1784, however, shows the same attraction for the quirky, apparent in the *Caprices*.

THE SLEEP OF REASON
1797; pen and sepia ink
In this drawing for the print *The Sleep of Reason Produces Monsters* (right), the draughtsman appears to be praying, rather than sleeping. Goya's face is among the demonic creatures oppressing him. The title is self-explanatory, given Goya's political cynicism at the time.

THE SLEEP OF REASON
1797–98; 21.5 x 15 cm (8¼ x 6 in); etching and aquatint
Goya first intended this image to be the title page for a series of prints entitled *Sueños* (dreams), to provide a logical context for the fanciful and nightmarish dream visions that followed. This is its final state, after going through several changes from the original image (left).

THERE THEY GO PLUCKED
1797–98; 21.5 x 15 cm (8½ x 5¼ in); etching and aquatint
This strange scene, set in a brothel, where prostitutes drive out their wretched clients, is Goya's comment on the increasing spread of syphilis. "Plucked" meant "fleeced", and could also mean "baldness" – a symptom of the disease, as was impotence, symbolized by the bandaged leg.

BLOW
1797–98; 21.5 x 15 cm (8½ x 5¼ in); etching and aquatint
This print's horrific depiction of paedophilic lust truly belongs to the realm of the nightmare. A tall male witch uses a child as a pair of "bellows", hence the work's title, while others look on. Another is shown sucking the penis of a small child. Babies are also being brought to the scene.

These illustrations are taken from a book, written in 1761, in which Goya could have found a complete guide to the most recent printing techniques.

LEANDRO FERNANDEZ MORATIN
1799; 73 x 56 cm (28¾ x 22 in)
Goya's friend, the playwright and poet Moratín, was also connected with the "enlightened" patrons of the arts, the Duke and Duchess of Osuna (pp. 30–31). Moratín was a radical liberal, well-travelled, and deeply antagonistic towards the forces of the Inquisition and the monarchy.

NOW THEY ARE SITTING PRETTY
1797–98; 21.5 x 15 cm (8½ x 5¼ in); etching and aquatint
A brilliant comic invention, this bizarre image is Goya's depiction of ignorant vanity. The two young victims of fashion display their foolishness and naivety by wearing their petticoats too short, and their *asientos* (which means seats or good sense) on their heads.

THOU WHO CANST NOT
1797–98; 21.5 x 15 cm (8½ x 5¼ in); etching and aquatint
Goya chose the ass, a symbol of stubborn stupidity, as a means of representing and attacking clerics and the richer classes. By showing asses saddled on the common people's backs, he criticizes their blind acceptance of the burden of social repression. One ass wears a spur.

PRINTING PRESS
This is the type of wooden, 18th-century printing press, which would have been used by Goya to transfer his engraved images onto paper.

Sorcery and witchcraft

GOYA'S PAINTINGS OF SORCERY AND WITCHCRAFT mark an important point in his development. Their darkly satirical, and even comic mood relates strongly to the *Caprices* series (pp. 28–29), which Goya was completing when he began his first series of six witchcraft paintings for the Duchess of Osuna's study. These small paintings evolved from Goya's Cabinet Pictures (pp. 24–25), where he permitted himself a free rein to express the fantasy side of his imagination, which had previously been restricted to his print-making. Sorcery and witchcraft were especially popular themes among playwrights and literary figures at this time, as they provided a vehicle for attacking the Holy Inquisition (pp. 44–45). For several centuries, the Inquisition had exploited the existence of superstitious beliefs to effectively terrorize and subdue the Spanish people, hindering the development of an enlightened Spain.

THE OSUNA PALACE, ALAMEDA
The Duke of Osuna purchased Goya's six small oil paintings of witchcraft and sorcery in 1798. They were commissioned by the Duchess for her study in their country residence at Alameda.

THE FAMILY OF THE DUKE OF OSUNA
1788; 225 x 174 cm (88½ x 68½ in)
The Duke and Duchess were enthusiastic and learned patrons of the arts, regularly opening their home to Spain's artists and intellectuals. Goya's perceptive and gentle family portrait is a masterpiece of colour harmony. Pink (a favourite colour of the Baroque period) is delicately balanced with jade green, and held together by the silver-grey tones that appear so often in Goya's paintings.

THE FORCIBLY BEWITCHED
c.1797–98; 42 x 30 cm (16½ x 11¾ in)
The subject of this painting is derived from a comic play entitled *The Devil's Lamp* by the 18th-century Spanish playwright, Antonio Zamora. This scene refers to a specific point in the play's narrative, which Goya appropriately chose to depict as if it were on a stage. In the bottom right-hand corner of the painting, portions of the text are placed so that they can be read – as though on a script held by a member of the audience. This passage in the play has as its main character a foolish and superstitious man, who thinks he has been forcibly bewitched and attempts to keep the devil's lamp alight, believing that if the lamp dies, so will he. He superstitiously covers his mouth, to prevent the devil from entering through it.

THE SPELL
1797–98; 45 x 32 cm (17½ x 12½ in)
This scene continues the theatrical feel of the Osuna paintings. The figures, which are casting spells, are grouped together in a dramatic formation. One of them is reading, as if from a script. Owls fly above the figures' heads. Witches and owls, in Spanish folklore, were supposed to be vampires that sucked blood.

Bosch's seven sins appear as individual narrative scenes

SEVEN DEADLY SINS
Hieronymous Bosch; 1475; 150 x 120 cm (59 x 47¼ in)
In 1570, King Philip II of Spain acquired seven works by the Flemish artist, Hieronymous Bosch (1450–1516). The *Seven Deadly Sins* was hung in his private room in the Escorial palace. By Goya's time, there existed in Spain a strong pictorial tradition, influenced by Bosch's grotesque supernatural inventions.

THE OWL
The original definition of "witch" in the Spanish language was a "nocturnal bird resembling the owl".

Owls feature strongly in Goya's witchcraft and anti-clerical works

PRETTY TEACHER
1797–98; 21.5 x 15 cm (8½ x 5¾ in); etching and aquatint
Ironically titled, this is one of several images in the *Caprices* series (pp. 28–29), depicting an old witch teaching a young attractive witch to fly. Flight had other connotations in 18th-century Spain (pp. 52–53). This image, for instance, refers to descriptions of witches and corrupt women servants teaching young, innocent girls about sexual pleasures.

THE WITCHES' SABBATH
1797–98; 44 x 31cm (17¼ x 12¼ in)
Goya returned to this theme in his Black Painting of the same name (pp. 50–51). In it, he transformed this work's brilliance of colour, dramatic light, and slightly foolish-looking he-goat into a genuinely dark image. For all the horror of its content, this painting is rather comic.

Goya's great fresco

Following his illness of 1792, Goya was unable to carry out any ambitious projects and was forced to concentrate on small works, such as his Cabinet Pictures and witchcraft scenes (pp. 24–25 & 30–31). By 1798, he had fallen into debt, and appealed to King Charles IV for work, attributing his financial difficulties to his deafness: "For six years I have been completely bereft of good health and in particular of my hearing, and I am so deaf that without using sign language I cannot understand anything." Goya's award of the commission to decorate the new church of San Antonio de la Florida in Madrid was a timely one, largely due to the influence of his friend, the statesman Jovellanos (pp. 28-29). It was a unique opportunity that allowed Goya an inordinate amount of freedom to interpret his subject – the miracle of St. Anthony of Padua. Situated on the Crown's land, the chapel's decoration did not come under the supervision of the Church.

San Antonio de la Florida

1798; 5.5 m diameter: (18 ft); fresco

As a decorative scheme, San Antonio is exceptional: a single narrative scene is depicted throughout the entire chapel. The miracle of St. Anthony is painted in the dome (above), and accompanying celebratory angels and cherubims appear on the arches and side walls.

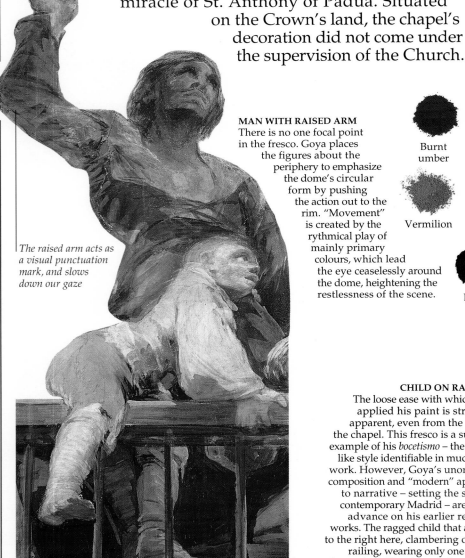

The raised arm acts as a visual punctuation mark, and slows down our gaze

MAN WITH RAISED ARM
There is no one focal point in the fresco. Goya places the figures about the periphery to emphasize the dome's circular form by pushing the action out to the rim. "Movement" is created by the rythmical play of mainly primary colours, which lead the eye ceaselessly around the dome, heightening the restlessness of the scene.

Burnt umber

Light red ochre

Earth green

Naples yellow

Lead white

Vermilion

Prussian blue

Black

RAPID FRESCO
The fluid, sketched quality of the paintings in San Antonio de la Florida owe much to Goya's use of fresco (p. 63), which demands speed of execution, since the paint must be applied while the plaster is still wet. Goya's practise was to outline his design on an initial layer of plaster, before finally painting in tempera on a top layer of plaster.

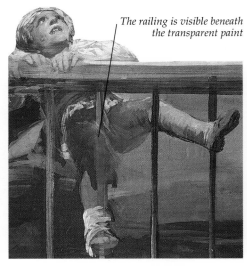

The railing is visible beneath the transparent paint

CHILD ON RAILINGS
The loose ease with which Goya applied his paint is strikingly apparent, even from the floor of the chapel. This fresco is a supreme example of his *bocetismo* – the sketch-like style identifiable in much of his work. However, Goya's unorthodox composition and "modern" approach to narrative – setting the scene in contemporary Madrid – are a great advance on his earlier religious works. The ragged child that appears to the right here, clambering over the railing, wearing only one shoe, is drawn from Goya's own observation.

This man's crudely formed face is almost indistinguishable

FIGURES IN THE CROWD

Goya presents us with a "real" crowd scene. There is a rejection of idealized form and conventional standards of beauty. His wide cross-section of people include not only the attractive – the colourful *majas,* for instance – but also the ugly, the poor, the deformed, and even the disreputable, in the form of the shadowy *celestina* (below right).

AN URBAN SCENE

Although this scene is set within sight of mountains, it is more urban than rural in character. Goya captures the presence of a gaggle of people by showing their attention being diverted in all directions. Some of the crowd express genuine wonderment, others a simple curiosity, and the rest a worldly indifference to the commotion caused by the dead man's resurrection (p. 32, top right).

Goya's fluid, rapid brushwork

Circular brushmarks emphasize the cylindrical form of an arm

ST. ANTHONY'S AUDIENCE

Despite the fresco's circular composition, Goya nevertheless succeeds in attracting our attention to the main figure of St. Anthony of Padua, dressed in a brown Franciscan habit (p. 32, top right). He did this pre-eminently through his portrayal of the response of the nearby crowd, who strain and peer over their shoulders for a glimpse of the saint.

The sinister figure of the celestina (p. 36)

The Royal Family

COURT LIFE UNDER KING CHARLES IV was utterly different from that of the previous monarch. While Charles III was austere and ascetic, leading a life of prayer, politics, and hunting, his son, Charles, and daughter-in-law, María Luisa, were self-indulgent, materially extravagant, and politically complacent. Charles IV was by all accounts a weak king, and María Luisa was accused of being vain and lascivious – a combination which led to their eventual downfall in 1808 (pp. 38–39). The Queen's alleged affair with Manuel Godoy (right) – the darling of the court, who was nationally detested – provoked widespread derision and contempt. In 1779, Goya, who by now had renewed contact with the Crown, was appointed to the highest position of First Court Painter. The following year, he produced his hugely ambitious and unorthodox portrait of the Royal Family.

THE ROYAL FAMILY
Painted on silk, this miniature by an unknown artist adopts a curious format. Charles IV and his family appear in profile, and the strong family likeness is accentuated.

MANUEL GODOY
1801; 180 x 267 cm (70¾ x 105 in)
Godoy began his career in the Royal Guard, and quickly become a favourite at court. By the age of 26, he was made Prime Minister of Spain, and, in 1795, after the Treaty of Basel, he was given the absurd title of "Prince of Peace". Goya portrayed him as an arrogant man, proud of his physical strength, against the backdrop of an encampment – a reference to Spain's war against Portugal, in 1801. Godoy's marriage to the Countess of Chinchón (left), was arranged by the Queen to give him royal connections.

MEDAL
The Bourbon kings loaded honours on their favourites.

THE COUNTESS OF CHINCHON
1800; 174 x 144 cm (68½ x 56½ in)
The Countess was the niece of Charles III, and daughter of Infante Don Luis (p. 18). Married in 1800 to Godoy, her cameo ring bears his portrait. This picture was painted when she was 21, and expecting her first child. The portrait may have been inspired by the Queen, who in her letters to Godoy took a special interest in the Countess' pregnancy. She seems a frail, unhappy young woman, and Goya has responded to her sad situation with great sensitivity.

FERTILITY SYMBOL
The young Countess wears ears of wheat in her hair, as a symbol of her fertility.

LAS MENINAS
Diego Velázquez; 1656; 318 x 276 cm (125 x 108½ cm)
This painting of the family and staff of Philip IV, held in the royal collections, provided a historical touchstone for any portrait that was later painted of the Spanish Royal Family. While Goya's vision is essentially different to Velázquez', the compact, frieze-like organization is a direct reference to *Las Meninas*.

INFANTE CARLOS MARIA ISIDRO
1800–01; 74 x 60 cm (29 x 23½ in); oil sketch
Goya made ten portrait studies from life, in preparation for his multi-figure portrait of the Royal Family (below). Large areas of the red-earth coloured ground, which were usually invisible below top layers of paint, have been left bare, since these compelling paintings were considered purely as sketches. This is a portrait study of the 12-year-old Infante Carlos María Isidro, who stands at the extreme left of the family composition.

INFANTA MARIA JOSEFA
1800–01; 74 x 60 cm (29 x 23½ in); oil sketch
Assuming a role of minor importance within the royal hierarchy was the aged sister of King Charles IV, who died shortly after this portrait was completed. Goya certainly never flattered his royal subjects, and she appears a slightly ridiculous figure with her feathered hairpiece and large jewellery. In the finished portrait, Goya showed even less compassion, sharpening her bird-like features and her resemblance to the king.

INFANTE FRANCISCO DE PAULA ANTONIO
1800–01; 74 x 60 cm (29 x 23½ in); oil sketch
While Goya's portrait of the aged Infanta Maria Josefa is a study of foolish vanity, his sympathetic portrayal of the six-year-old Infante Francisco de Paula Antonio exhibits a natural and unselfconscious beauty. This half-painted oil sketch helps to illustrate Goya's method of applying paint to the canvas. The area of red, describing his trousers, is a "negative" image, where the red-earth ground has been left bare and Goya has painted the space around the child.

THE FAMILY OF CHARLES IV
1800–01; 280 x 336 cm (110¼ x 132¼ in)
This painting's dazzling combination of yellow, grey, and blue, interspersed with luminous vermilion (red), is unified by a "cobweb" of silver-grey running across the picture, describing contours and ornamentation on the clothing. The figure of the King is exceptional, both for his rich brown suit and his totally vacant gaze – matched only by his sister's (above left). They seem hollow characters, defined by their overwhelming materialism, and, for all their splendour, present a strangely intimate scene. The portrayal of the Infanta Dona María Luisa Josefina is unusually informal – she is shown carrying her baby. María Luisa assumes a central position, her stance echoing that of the young Infanta in *Las Meninas*. The future Ferdinand VII (p. 45), opposite the King, stands next to his future wife, whose face remains hidden. Goya's subordinate position, behind the family, reinforces the royal hierarchy and also suggests that he painted the portrait from their mirror image.

Majas and majismo

THE *MAJA* WAS AN EXCLUSIVELY SPANISH, particularly urban, character. Her male counterpart, the *majo*, was the Spanish equivalent of the dandy, with a good deal more bravado. They were both streetwise, colourful, and provocative, instantly recognizable by their demeanour and their dress. A *maja* could be identified by her tight bodice with sleeves, lace mantilla, and overtly sexual, flirtatious manner; a *majo* wore a narrow-waisted jacket, white stockings, a voluminous cloak, and broad-brimmed hat. In 1766, Charles III's minister, Marchese di Squillace, attempted to outlaw the *majo*'s notorious cloak, because of its ability to conceal weapons and enable thieves to "disappear". The *majismo* lifestyle greatly appealed to fashionable society women, who had traditionally followed French dress codes, but now developed a taste for dressing up as "common" *majas*. Queen María Luisa (right), and her rival in fashion, the Duchess of Alba (pp. 26–27), both sported the *majismo* look. One of Goya's most striking portraits is of the beautiful Dona Isabel de Porcel dressed as a *maja*.

THE MAJA'S CELESTINA
Goya's *majas* are often shown with a celestina, an aged procuress, as in this *Caprices* etching (pp. 28–29), *It is Well Pulled Up*. The celestina looks on approvingly as the girl arranges her stockings.

MARIA LUISA IN A MANTILLA
1799; 210 x 130 cm (82½ x 51 in)
In a xenophobic age, the influence of the Italian-born Queen over Charles IV was extremely unpopular. This portrait, showing María Luisa dressed as a *maja*, can be regarded as an attempt to portray her as a natural Spaniard.

NAKED MAJA
c.1798–1805; 97 x 190 cm (38 x 74¾ in)
The female nude is rare in Spanish art. Goya's treatment of the taboo subject, however, remains one of the most uncompromisingly honest and sexually provocative in art history. (It was the first to include female pubic hair).

CLOTHED MAJA
c.1798–1805; 95 x 190 cm (37¼ x 74¾ in)
The *Clothed Maja* escaped the awkward joining of the head to the body, evident in its counterpart (above). For all the *Naked Maja*'s overt sexuality, the *Clothed Maja* is more erotic. In 1815, both were confiscated from their owner, Godoy (pp. 34–35), by the Inquisition, and Goya was faced with obscenity charges.

FAN
This elaborately decorated 18th-century Spanish fan reveals the extent to which French fashions were adopted in Spain. The figures, who are shown in a Spanish street, wear costumes that are recognisably French.

X-RAY PHOTOGRAPH
An x-ray photograph of the portrait of *Dona Isabel de Porcel* shows how it was painted over an existing portrait by Goya. This was only discovered when the painting needed re-lining, and it was x-rayed.

Dona Isabel de Porcel

1804–05; 82 x 54 cm (32¼ x 21¼ in)
This portrait is a brilliant example of Goya's masterful use of ivory black. Goya's "Spanish black" has its own history. It influenced the French painter Edouard Manet (1832–83) and the 20th-century Abstract Expressionist, Robert Motherwell (1915–), who exploited it in his huge *Elegies to Spain*.

PAINTED FACE
Isabel de Porcel's highly defined lips and eyes suggest that she was heavily made-up for her portrait, possibly by Goya. He did this for the Duchess of Alba, when she sat for him (p. 27).

CONTRASTING FORM
This painting is a masterpiece of rose and black. The mantilla, which has all the crisp delicacy of fine lace, contrasts against Isabel de Porcel's pale, aristocratic skin, creating a dazzling effect.

THEATRICAL MOOD
The dynamic sweep of the mantilla, and alert, theatrical pose suggest that energetic action has been held suspended for a moment: the sitter appears a palpably real, breathing person.

The guerilla war

BY DECEMBER 1807, FRANCE had been at war with Britain for over four years. With Manuel Godoy's blessing, Napoleon marched 130,000 French troops into northern Spain on the pretext of protecting his Spanish allies from a British invasion. During the spring of 1808, French troops entered Madrid, effectively taking control of the city. When angry riots against Godoy threatened the safety of Charles IV, he handed over the Crown to his son and fled Madrid. Ferdinand VII, however, was king for little more than a month before being exiled (pp. 40–42). On 6 June 1808, Napoleon declared his brother, Joseph, King of Spain (p. 41), and the guerilla war between the Spanish and the occupying force began. Although Goya did go on to receive commissions from Joseph I and Ferdinand VII, the war destroyed the old order of Bourbon patronage for him, and he started to turn his attention away from the Court to pursue his own private work.

NAPOLEON AND GODOY SATIRE
In this contemporary allegorical print, which resembles Goya's *Sleep of Reason* (p. 28), Godoy's sleep brings forth the monsters of war.

THE SECOND OF MAY 1808
The events of this day, when Spanish crowds attempted to prevent the Royal Family leaving the Palace in Madrid, became symbolic of the Spanish people's resistance to the French. Goya celebrated it in his painting of 1814 (p. 43).

ALLEGORY OF THE TOWN OF MADRID
1810; 260 x 195 cm (102¼ x 76¾ in)
This unusual painting has a colourful history. It was originally commissioned by the Madrid City Council for their town hall during the brief reign of the usurper king, Joseph I. Goya painted it in the Classical-Baroque style, suited to the imperialistic pretensions of the Bonapartist regime. The oval shield or plaque, which at first bore Joseph I's portrait, was replaced after his downfall with the word *constitución* (referring to the Cadiz Constitution). It was later over-painted with an image of Ferdinand VII, and again in 1872 with the existing, patriotic inscription *Dos de Mayo* (second of May).

MAKING SHOT IN THE SIERRA
c.1810–14; 33 x 52 cm (12¾ x 20½ in); oil on panel
This is one of two small panels that Goya painted, showing guerillas making shot and powder in Aragon. Panel was a cheaper surface to paint on than canvas, which suggests that Goya was having difficulty obtaining artists' materials at the time, particularly for his private works. In Spanish, *guerrilla* means "little war", but however small this war was by military standards, it had devastating consequences for the Spanish people (pp. 40–41).

SHEEP'S HEAD AND JOINTS
c.1808–12; 45 x 62 cm (17¾ x 24¼ in)
This startling image belongs to a series of paintings, largely of game, butchered meat, and fish. There is an undeniable brutality in the few still lifes Goya produced, perhaps due to his state of mind during the war. They were painted at about the same time as his small genre "horror" paintings (below).

SAVAGES MURDERING A WOMAN
c.1808–14; 29 x 41 cm (11¼ x 16 in); oil on tin plate
In this period of conflict, Goya produced works with intensely violent or sadistic themes, doubly disturbing for their contrast with the delicate painted surfaces.

THE COLOSSUS
c.1808–12; 116 x 105 cm (45½ x 41¼ in)
The giant appears at its most enigmatic in Goya's *Colossus*; variously interpreted as an allegory of war or as Spain's terrible avenger. The painting's strange, silent, dream-like quality, and mixture of reality and unreality has a mesmeric effect. The giant appears somnambulant, oblivious to the terror he inspires; only a donkey, standing stock-still amidst the panic, remains unmoved. *Colossus* is beautifully painted. Most notable of all is the grey-pink scudding cloud, thickly applied with a palette knife dragged into the grey-blue sky.

THE COLOSSUS
c.1810–18; 28.5 x 21 cm (11¼ x 8¼ in); mezzotint
This is a calmer, more elusive counterpart to Goya's earlier painting of the same subject (left). Here, the giant rests alone on the horizon, appearing weary and dispirited under a night sky.
A very beautiful work, it is Goya's only mezzotint (p. 63).

The horrors of war

MURDER OF A FRENCH SOLDIER
This naive, anonymous print is contemporary to *The Disasters of War*.

THE CONTINUING WAR between Spanish civilians and French troops meant that Goya received fewer commissions and was freer to articulate his responses to the conflict. In 1810, when Goya began his second great series of prints, *The Disasters of War*, fighting had reached new levels of ferocity. The violent events of the 2nd and 3rd of May, 1808 (pp. 38 & 43), which had triggered the civilian uprising against the occupying enemy, set a pattern for the entire war, as atrocity was met with worse atrocity on both sides. Despite the cruelty practised against Spanish guerilla fighters, the French passed liberal reforms allowing greater freedom than under Spanish rule. It was the underlying messages of these barbaric images that Goya hoped would appeal to reason.

THE "DESIRED ONE"
This is an engraving by Vicente López (p. 60) of Ferdinand VII – who granted only 45-minute sittings to his Court Painters.

This is What you Were Born For

c.1810–12; 16 x 23.5 cm (6¼ x 9¼ in); etching and lavis
Goya produced his *Disasters of War* series over a decade, continuing work on it for six years after the war had ended. The series divides into three main groups: the war, the famine year 1811–12, and the *caprichos enfaticos* (striking caprices), which were violently anti-clerical. The incriminating anti-establishment tone of the images, evident in this war etching, meant that the copperplates had to be kept under lock and key until 26 years after Goya's death in 1828.

AND THEY ARE LIKE WILD BEASTS
c.1812–15; 15.5 x 21 cm (6 x 8¼ in); etching and aquatint
A royal decree of 1809 called for townsfolk to "make use of stones, sticks, etc., in the absence of other weapons" against the enemy. Goya's etching illustrates the futility and inevitable outcome of misguided action: the naked baby emphasizes the women's disadvantaged position.

THEY DON'T WANT TO
c.1810–15; 15.5 x 21cm (6 x 8¼ in); etching and aquatint
The old woman, no longer a target for rape, attempts to divert the danger away from the young girl. The frightened girl is no match for the soldier, but the old woman, with the self-possession of her long experience, attacks the soldier with ferocious contempt.

USURPER KING
Joseph Bonaparte became King Joseph I of Spain on 20 June 1808, at the instigation of his brother Napoleon Bonaparte, Emperor of France. Joseph wrote to Napoleon shortly after he had usurped the Spanish throne, "My position is unique: I have not a single supporter".

ETCHED PLATE FOR LO MISMO
This deeply etched plate reveals Goya's incredible surety of line. It also shows how the process of printing reverses the design on a plate – flipping the originally etched image.

THIS IS WORSE
c.1812–15; 15.5 x 20.5 cm (6 x 8 in); etching and lavis
During the war, naked corpses of guerilla fighters were mutilated, dismembered, and left hanging or impaled on trees as examples to the Spanish people. This image of such an age-old, demoralizing tactic, however, is so horrific that it suspends belief, despite its accuracy.

LO MISMO (THE SAME)
c.1810–15; 16 x 22 cm (6¼ x 8½ in); etching and lavis
Here, desperate civilians are forced to fight a sophisticated enemy with the only tools they have to hand. The peasant's anguished face personifies the brutalizing effects of war. He appears horrified by his own actions, in the helpless knowledge that in destroying his enemy he likewise destroys himself.

NOTHING. THE EVENT WILL TELL
c.1812–20; 15.5 x 20 cm (6 x 7¾ in); etching and aquatint
As one of Goya's "striking caprices", this grim work expresses his disillusionment with the reactionary restoration forces (pp. 42–45). After the terrible sacrifices and hardships suffered by the Spaniards, the corpse writes on a piece of paper the rewards due to them in peacetime: "Nothing".

THERE IS NO ONE TO HELP HIM
c.1812–15; 15.5 x 20.5 cm (6 x 8 in); etching and aquatint
This painful image of a dying man, overcome with grief at the plight of his family, is one of the series that records the famine that struck Spain in 1811. There is no comfort to be had here from the barren landscape, and the starving man stands like a frail monument to universal suffering.

Spanish rule restored

Having overthrown the Spanish Monarchy in 1808, and installed his brother Joseph as King Joseph I of Spain, Napoleon continued his campaign southwards, invading Portugal in 1809. On 22 July 1812, the British Duke of Wellington defeated the French army at Salamanca, in western Spain. By June the following year, a further British victory at Vitoria, in the north, brought an end to French occupation. The exiled Spanish King, Ferdinand VII, returned to Madrid to the great joy of the Spanish people. He, however, proved to be a cruel and reactionary dictator, who brought with him a new nightmare. His revival of the Inquisition led to a redoubled persecution of the liberals. Goya was reinstated as Painter to the King, in spite of his antipathy towards Ferdinand. It was not until 1814 that Goya painted his memorials to the uprising against the French of 2 May, 1808, and the consequent executions of the insurgents on 3 May, 1808.

ALLEGORY OF THE TRIUMPH OF SPAIN
This engraving allegorises Ferdinand VII's triumphant return to the throne, in May 1814. He is depicted entering Madrid on a chariot, passing through a triumphal arch, accompanied by virtues and cherubs. The cherubs carry a Union Jack, emphasizing the British role in the restoration.

ALLEGORY OF WELLINGTON
This contemporary engraving was printed in London to celebrate Wellington's victories in Spain. The text on the left eulogises the battle at Salamanca, and that on the right the victory at Vitoria.

THE DUKE OF WELLINGTON
1812–14; 60 x 51 cm (23½ x 20 in); oil on panel
This portrait of the Duke of Wellington posed enormous difficulties for Goya. In addition to the many decorations Wellington already possessed, he was awarded several more for his victories in Spain. These decorations, in the form of medals and sashes of varying shape and size, had to be continually added to the portrait, according to Wellington's wishes. In the end, the Duke did not like the painting, despite the profound intelligence of Goya's portrayal of him.

DUKE OF WELLINGTON
1812; 23 x 17.5 cm (9 x 6¾ in); red chalk over pencil
This sensitive drawing is one of two that Goya did of Wellington. It reveals a tired, melancholy man – more human and vulnerable than that of the official portrait. Goya's portraits of the Duke were painted after the battle of Arapiles in August 1812, and after his triumph in Madrid.

SELF-PORTRAIT
1815; 51 x 46 cm
(20 x 18 in); oil on panel
At 69, Goya had been deaf for 23 years, widowed for three, and summoned before the Inquisition on obscenity charges (p. 36). In this painting of great honesty, we can see his enduring determination.

THIRD OF MAY 1808
1814; 266 x 345 cm
(104½ x 135¾ in)
After the uprising of 2 May 1808, French soldiers executed Spanish insurgents across Madrid. This stark, brutal portrayal went on to influence Edouard Manet's and Pablo Picasso's paintings of war and political strife.

Second of May 1808

1814; 266 x 345 cm (104½ x 135¾ in)
Three months before Ferdinand's return, Goya's petition to the King declared his wish to commemorate the "most notable and heroic actions or scenes of our glorious insurrection against the tyrant of Europe". By this show of patriotic zeal, Goya probably hoped to escape punishment for earlier incriminating services to the "tyrant of Europe" (p. 38).

MUTILATED BODY
The considerably distorted, twisted head and oddly foreshortened body of the dead man (bottom left), creates a strikingly honest image of violent death.

VIOLENT REALISM
Contrary to the artistic tradition that encouraged the glorification of war, Goya produced a chaotic, journalistic "snap-shot" image of desperate violence.

ROMANTIC INFLUENCE
Goya's dramatic portrayal of street fighting inspired the French Romantic artist Eugéne Delacroix (1798–1863). This is clearly evident in works such as his *Arab Skirmishes*.

TRANSPARENT PAINT
This painting, of Goya's middle phase, is surprisingly thinly painted. It is tonally unified by the red-earth coloured ground, which is clearly visible beneath the surface.

Goya and the Church

FOR BEING A LIBERAL?
Goya's drawings attacking the
persecution of liberals are his
strongest political statement.
This immensely powerful
image of a woman, dazed
with exhaustion, suggests
her terrible ordeal.

AFTER THE WAR, the reinstated king, Ferdinand VII (right), systematically persecuted liberals and reformers. The restoration of the Inquisition caused widespread political confusion, and the mass exodus of intellectuals from Spain, including Goya's friend Moratín (p. 58). Having been cleared of collaboration with the enemy during the war, Goya resumed work at Court. Although short-lived, this seemingly mercenary standpoint of Goya's is hard to explain – it can only be supposed that his fear of poverty was stronger than his political beliefs. Tastes had changed, and academic artists like Vicente López were now popular (p. 60). Goya concentrated his energies completely on private works, such as his darkly satirical anti-clerical panel paintings (below). It was a shift that anticipated his final withdrawal from society, in 1816.

PROCESSION OF THE FLAGELLANTS
c.1812–19; 46 x 73 cm (18 x 28½ in); oil on panel
Here, Goya satirizes the grotesque aspect of penitential rituals. His image of the scene is an exaggerated and out-moded one: stripped to the waist and bleeding, the flagellants wear the tall conical hats of accused heretics (below). This type of spectacle was outlawed in 1777, by Charles III.

DEVOTIONAL SYMBOL
Through excessive displays of penitence, the flagellants (below) identified their self-inflicted suffering with Christ's sacrifice on the cross, and thus hoped to inspire faith.

INQUISITION SCENE
c.1812–19; 46 x 73 cm (18 x 28½ in); oil on panel
This painting was probably based on descriptions of the famous witch trials of the *auto-de-fé* (act of faith) of the Spanish Inquisition in 1610. Goya was undoubtedly familiar with Moratín's satirical account of them. He seems to be drawing parallels between the barbaric practices of ancient witch-trials and the flouting of human liberties, exercised in his own contemporary Spain. Here, the accused are wearing *Sambenitos*, garments that publicly advertise the nature of their crimes.

KING FERDINAND VII WITH ROYAL MANTLE
1814; 212 x 146 cm (83½ x 57½ in)
This is one of several portraits of the king, painted from memory, and from the preparatory drawings that Goya made for the original equestrian portrait of him. Ferdinand VII, ironically named *El Deseado*, "The Desired One", was a ruthless reactionary, who in the aftermath of the French revolution and invasion of Spain viewed the liberal *afrancesados*, as his enemies.

THE CARNIVOROUS VULTURE
c.1815–20; 17.5 x 22 cm (6¾ x 8½ in); etching
This over-sized, grotesque bird is Goya's allegory for the Holy Inquisition. Squawking and flapping, it is driven away by a sturdy-looking peasant.

AGAINST THE COMMON GOOD
c.1815–20; 17.5 x 22 cm (6¾ x 8½ in); etching
Another symbol of the corrupt church, this Holy man with huge bat ears sits on a globe representing the world, busily writing in a large book.

THE BURIAL OF THE SARDINE
1812–19; 82.5 x 62 cm (32½ x 24¼ in); oil on panel
At first glance, this picture seems to depict the happy subject of a carnival procession. However, the carnival no longer took place in Goya's lifetime so that the painting depicts an imagined "historical" time and has more sinister implications. The mass of swarming figures, punctuated by masks of death heads and beasts, lend the crowd an undertone of menace, and the potential of a wild mob. The huge grinning mask on the banner, appears as a mascot for madness, chaos, and degeneracy. This uninhibited scene represents the antithesis of the enlightened years of rule under Charles III (p. 20).

A woman's carnival mask

A bird-like mask

MASKS
Grotesque masks were worn by revellers in the ritualistic Ash Wednesday carnival (right), which ended with the ritualized burial of the "sardine" – a symbol for the beginning of Lent. Originally, it was a pig rather than a fish that was buried. These masks have been recreated from the painting.

Brush with death

AT THE END OF 1819, WHEN GOYA WAS 73, he became seriously ill and very nearly died. The old illness, which had left him totally deaf in 1792 (pp. 24–25), returned with a vengeance. Goya attributed his survival to the care and skill of his physician. On his recovery the following year, he expressed his gratitude in this great painting, *Self-portrait with Dr. Arrieta*. By publicly exposing his own feeble, agitated condition, Goya cast his doctor in the role of hero. The combined drama and pathos created an immensely moving work. Goya's illness had occurred shortly after his completion of an altarpiece, *The Last Communion of St. Joseph of Calasanz*, for the Escuelas Pías de San Antón in Madrid. Parallel in theme to Goya's self-portrait, it highlighted Goya's own resistance to death. Whereas St. Joseph of Calasanz is shown to meet his death in serene readiness, the artist depicted himself struggling for life – literally clinging onto his bedclothes. Before his illness, Goya bought a country house outside Madrid, the House of the Deaf Man (p. 48), where he spent his convalescence.

Raw umber   Vermilion   Light red   Lead white

Terre verte

Prussian blue

Ivory black

CHANGING PALETTE
As Goya matured, his palette grew increasingly sombre. This painting exhibits characteristics of his middle phase, sharing a similar paint consistency and handling to the *Second* and *Third of May 1808*, for instance (p. 43). It also shows signs of his imminent departure into his last great phase – the Black Paintings (pp. 48–55).

Self-portrait with Dr. Arrieta

1820; 117 x 79 cm (46 x 31 in)

The painting's varied and uneven surface, made up of contrasting areas of *impasto* (p. 63) and thin transparent paint, introduces Goya's late phase of painting. The new rawness of this work is characteristic of his later Black Paintings. *Self-Portrait with Dr. Arrieta* is interesting for its juxtaposition of loose, broad, brushwork and reduced definition with tight drawing and compact compositional arrangement. The luminosity of the red counterpane and brilliant white of Goya's nightshirt serve to distract us, initially, from the sinister figures lurking in the shadows behind the bed.

SELF-PORTRAIT

The solid white of the night-shirt worn by Goya creates a central focus. The paint is applied in thick strokes of unmixed lead white, which attracts any light falling onto the surface. Conversely, Goya's head – painted so thinly that the bare canvas shows through – appears to be fading into the gloom. His dull unhealthy pallor and translucent skin are highlighted by the sharp whiteness of the night-shirt. The artist's helpless condition is made all the more poignant by his doctor's determined solicitation, symbolized by his strong arm moving the medicine towards Goya's mouth. Goya drifts towards the shadows, losing consciousness, while his doctor leans forward, supporting his weight, creating tension and counterbalance.

GHOSTLY ATTENDANTS

The figures in the shadows behind Goya and his doctor have an air of implacable patience, like dogs waiting for the chance to steal scraps from a table. (The figure, to the left here, holds a letter.) These people were probably Goya's attendants or friends, but the purpose of their presence is ambiguous, as they take on the role of harbingers of death. They appear less than life-size, in an undefined space behind the sick-bed. Their obscurity in the shadows, together with Goya's semi-delirious state suggests that they were intended to be read as an imagined presence. This is reminiscent of his *Caprices* print, *The Sleep of Reason*, (p. 28).

INSUBSTANTIAL FORM

One of the figures, which is barely visible behind the bed, is thought to be Goya's housekeeper, Leocardia Zorilla. All insubstantial beings, the shades lurking in the depths of the picture belong to the realm of the phantom. Their presence, juxtaposed with that of Goya and his doctor, emphasizes the foreground figures' mortality, by making them appear weightier and more solid.

GOYA'S DEDICATION TO DR. ARRIETA

The painting's inscription reads: "Goya, in gratitude to his friend Arrieta: for the compassion and care with which he saved his life in his acute and dangerous illness, suffered at the end of 1819 at the age of 73. He painted this in 1820". Arrieta, a fashionable doctor in Madrid, was later dispatched to Africa to study the bubonic plague.

House of the Deaf Man

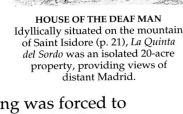

HOUSE OF THE DEAF MAN
Idyllically situated on the mountain of Saint Isidore (p. 21), *La Quinta del Sordo* was an isolated 20-acre property, providing views of distant Madrid.

IN 1819, WHILE OFFICIALLY retaining his title as First Painter to King Ferdinand VII, Goya decided to withdraw from society completely, to view the political upheavals in Madrid from the distance of his quiet country home – the House of the Deaf Man. (The name of the house ironically referred to a previous occupant). Following the uprising led by General Riego on 1 January 1820, the King was forced to accept the conditions laid down by the liberals. On 4 April, Goya attended the Royal Academy in Madrid for the last time, with the sole purpose of swearing his allegiance to the new liberal constitution. There then ensued an era of newborn optimism for Spain as the Inquisition was abolished and prisoners from the old regime were released. The reality, however, was one of continued unrest, and this brief period of liberalism came to represent the quiet before the storm (pp. 56–57). At the beginning of 1820, Goya began an extraordinary project that was to occupy him for the next three years – the decoration of two rooms of his house with the strange and brilliant series that was to be immortalized as the Black Paintings (shown here, and also on pp. 50–55).

YOUNG WOMAN WITH A LETTER
c.1808-12; 181 x 125 cm (71¼ x 48 in)
The beautiful young woman, in this earlier painting, is thought to be Leocadia Zorilla, at about 24 years old, after her separation from her husband.

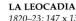

LA LEOCADIA
1820–23; 147 x 132 cm (5⁷⁄₄ x 51¾ in); oil on plaster
Goya's mistress, Leocadia Zorilla, lived with Goya in the House of the Deaf Man, as his housekeeper. *La Leocadia* was painted at the first doorway of a ground-floor room, where some of the Black Paintings were housed. Goya's inclusion of a tomb, and his adornment of Leocadia in mourning, combine to create an air of melancholy, suggesting that this painting was intended as a frontispiece to the hellish themes of the Black Paintings – setting them in the context of a world beyond the grave. The rough swirls of the house's plaster, on which it was originally painted, are still visible in its surface.

THE DOG
1820–23; 134 x 80 cm (52½ x 31½ in); oil on plaster
This strange, sad painting, from the upper floor of the house, shows a small dog either buried in sand or peering over a shadowy ridge at some unseen menace. Whatever the case, the imagery is ominous. The identity of the shadowy form, looming dimly in the surrounding space, is a mystery.

DUEL WITH CUDGELS
*1820–23; 123 x 266 cm
(48¼ x 104½ in); oil on plaster*
Here two men – possibly
brothers – are shown
fighting with heavy cudgels
– slowly, rhythmically as
though they are driving a
post. Their legs disappear
into the ground, like Goya's
Colossus, yet they appear
wedded to the land; and
so their fight must be to
the death. Bitter clashes
between monarchists and
liberals in northern Spain,
at this time, imply that
Goya may have intended
this painting as an
allegory of civil war.

FEVERISH STROKES
The feverish energy
of Goya's late brushwork
is evident in Tío Paquete's
dome-like forehead. The
thickly *impastoed* paint (p.
63), compulsively applied,
attracts light falling on to
the painted surface,
thereby emphasizing
the spherical form.

VISIBLE CHANGES
During the course
of painting this portrait,
Goya reduced the size of
Tío's head to this compact
form. This appears as a
pentimento (a correction
clearly visible through the
picture surface) above
the contours of the
old beggar's head.

DUAL VISION
Tío's similarity
to some of Goya's more
grotesque figures delays
a sympathetic reading.
Goya counteracted this
caricature-like treatment
of Tío by suggesting his
indomitable spirit –
another example of the
duality of Goya's vision.

Tío Paquete

c.1820–23; 39 x 31 cm (15¼ x 12¼ in)

This portrait of the celebrated blind beggar/singer, Tío
Paquete suggests a parody of Goya's own self-portrait,
aged 69 (p. 43). Alike in clothing and palette, the heads
are shown similarly tilted. Goya's deafness, in his later
years, undoubtedly revealed another world to him, and
here he seems to have portrayed Tío as a caricature of
his own infirmity. Tío's expressive grin appears in
several other works, most notably on the head of the
carnival banner in *The Burial of the Sardine* (p. 45) and on
the face of the carnival idiot, Bobalicón (p. 56).

The Black Paintings

GOYA PRODUCED PREPARATORY SKETCHES for all 14 Black Paintings before painting them in oils directly onto the plaster walls of the large dining-room and salon of his house. This oil-based *al secco* technique (p. 63) had replaced fresco by the early 19th century, as its slow-drying properties allowed for alterations and greater spontaneity. Goya probably decorated the salon first, exploring diverse subjects with a varied palette. He, however, centred the ground-floor dining-room on *Saturn*, revealing a synthesis of horror, powerfully dark in both theme and colour. Throughout, Goya combined the monumental scale of his religious frescoes with the highly personal vision of works such as *The Proverbs* (p. 56), so that in his 74th year he produced his last and greatest surge of creativity, which gave full vent to his pessimism and misanthropy.

TWO OLD MEN
*1820–23; 144 x 66 cm
(56½ x 25¾ in); oil on plaster*
An aged, bearded man listens wearily, as a younger man with grotesque features shouts into his ear. The meaning, however, is ambiguous: is this a parody of deafness and old age, or a portrayal of a sinister adviser?

TWO OLD PEOPLE EATING
*1820–23; 53 x 85 cm
(20¾ x 33½ in); oil on plaster*
Goya painted this, for his dining-room. One crone (or witch) spoons broth, while her skeletal companion looks on. Their bony fingers are painted in single brushstrokes.

SATURN DEVOURING HIS SONS
1797–98; red chalk
The Roman god Saturn (or Cronus, the ancient Greek deity) devoured his children who, it was prophesized, would usurp his power.

SATURN
1820–23; 146 x 83 cm (57½ x 32½ in); oil on plaster
Goya's Saturn suggests a regression to primal savagery. However, the distinctly adult proportions of the child's body – despite the obscenity of the image – turns the mythological horror story into a symbol of uncontrolled violence and abused power. Unlike Rubens's painting (right), our sympathy is deflected from the now anonymous corpse, towards Saturn. He appears insane, driven by desperation to devour his own children. In trying to escape his fate, he brings on his own destruction.

SATURN
Peter Paul Rubens; 1686; 180 x 87 cm (70¾ x 34¼ in)
Rubens's Saturn, though outwardly more refined than Goya's, remains the more horrific of the two. The viewer's sympathy is directed towards the baby, yet to be eaten, and Saturn appears a cruel, corrupt power. Afraid of losing his great strength, he seems remorseless, unaware of the ghostly figure of death behind him.

The Great He-Goat

1820–23; 140 x 438 cm (55 x 172¼ in); oil on plaster
The subject of this painting is a reworking of Goya's earlier picture *The Witches Sabbath* (p. 31). However, this version, is more truly sinister, set at night in an open landscape, where the devil conducts a mass for his bestial congregation.

MAJA
At the far right, sitting on a chair, facing the he-goat, is a young *maja*, possibly the subject of the devil's interest. The others sit on the ground, bare-footed.

CONGREGATION
Among the hideous gathering are many bestial faces. However, they remain human, open-mouthed, and gullible.

HE-GOAT
The crowd is animated – faces peer in all directions. Some appear excited by the he-goat, who in contrast to his audience is not only immobile and silhouetted, but also has his activity concealed.

OLD WOMAN
The old woman on the far left, who has her head bowed and her legs stretched out in front of her, is either deeply engrossed in prayer, or fast asleep.

Beasts of the air

FLYING IS SYNONYMOUS WITH WITCHES and supernatural creatures, which is why Goya probably depicted his fantastic creations in mid-flight. By attributing to them such non-human qualities, he greatly increased their power to unsettle the spectator. Flying, levitating, or rising through the air was a common symbol for sexual pleasure, or the sexual act in 18th-century Spain; the word "flying" also had the additional slang meaning "to rob". Earlier, Goya had used such imagery in his *Caprices* etchings of 1799 (pp. 28–29), which were censored by the Inquisition, and in his witchcraft paintings of the following year (pp. 30–31). The main function of such imagery was the evocation of depravity and evil. These dark themes were Goya's overwhelming preoccupation towards the end of his life. But the idea of human flight, aside from its associated symbolic meaning, had clearly also captured his imagination. He may have witnessed early aviation attempts, such as the one that possibly inspired his satirical etching *A Way of Flying* (bottom right). His landscape of 1812–16, *The Balloon*, depicted a hot-air balloon in flight – a recent invention at the beginning of the 19th century.

VISION (above)
c.1820–23; 20 x 48.5 cm (7¾ x 19 in); oil sketch
This is Goya's rapidly executed sketch for the mysterious *Asmodea* (below), one of the pictures in the first-floor salon of the House of the Deaf Man. The figures in it resemble those in *Duel with Cudgels*, also from the same room (p. 48). The soldiers, who are in the final painting, do not appear here. The figures being violently hurled about in the air are calmer in the final version.

ASMODEA (below)
1820–23; 123 x 266 cm (48½ x 104¾ in); oil on plaster
Despite its nightmare imagery this is a radiantly beautiful painting. It is infused with golden tones, interspersed with blue-silver, which are broken up by two isolated areas of red. The massive rock appears hazy and insubstantial beside the solid mass of the two figures flying by. It is not clear whether the two soldiers are shooting at them or at the distant horsemen.

THE FATES
1820–23; 123 x 266 cm (48½ x 104½ in); oil on plaster
The Fates takes its theme from Greek mythology. Clotho, Lachesis, and Atropos were thought to command birth, human events, and death, respectively. In accordance with this, Clotho was associated with a distaff (a cleft stick used in winding wool for spinning), Lachesis a spindle, and Atropos a pair of shears. Goya's painting, however, only corresponds partly with this mythology, and he has added a fourth figure.

The painting's steely winter light, cold colour range, and eerie, night landscape creates a deeply menacing image, reminiscent of the witching hour.

A WAY OF FLYING
c.1815–20; 24.5 x 35 cm (9½ x 13½ in); etching and aquatint
From 1815–24, Goya produced a remarkable series of prints on the subject of folly or absurdity, *Los Disparates*, also known as *Los Proverbios* (proverbs). The frequently sinister and bizarre mood of this series, also relates to works, such as *Asmodea* (left), that he painted on the walls of his house (pp. 50–51). Like them, they were made for his own satisfaction.

RIDICULOUS FOLLY
c.1815–24; 24.5 x 35 cm (9½ x 13½ in); etching and aquatint
This bizarre image of a group of seemingly oblivious figures perched precariously on the end of a dead branch, belongs to Goya's *Follies (Los Disparates)* series.

A WAY OF FLYING
1815–20; 24.5 x 35 cm (9½ x 13½ in) red chalk
This chalk and wash drawing is Goya's blue-print for his etching *A Way of Flying* (above).

It differs from the others in the series, for it appears to be based on reality, as opposed to pure fantasy.

A muted world

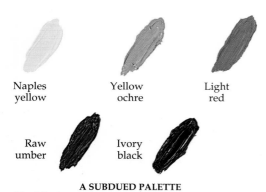

Naples
yellow

Yellow
ochre

Light
red

Raw
umber

Ivory
black

GOYA'S MACABRE PAINTING of the feast day of Saint
Isidore is often regarded as a dark parody of his work
The Meadow of Saint Isidore, painted over 30 years earlier
(p. 20). It is uncertain, however, whether this later painting
relates to the same festivities, as it was given its current title
after Goya's death. Nevertheless, it certainly depicts some
form of religious procession, for monks' shaved heads can
be identified amid the crush. Goya used "printing black"
– stiff, glutinous ink used by print-makers – in his Black
Paintings. This is known to cause excessive darkening, and
consequently these paintings appear substantially blacker
today than when they were painted. In 1873, the paintings'
deteriorating condition caused them to be removed from the
walls of the House of the Deaf Man (pp. 48–49) for restoration
– a drastic move necessitating the
house's demolition. Using the transfer
method, each painting was faced
with a temporary canvas, and the
walls behind them taken down. Once
the plaster was exposed, another
canvas was permanently fixed to
the reverse surface, and the painting
removed. The facing canvas was
then peeled away to reveal the picture.

The Pilgrimage of Saint Isidore

1820–23; 140 x 438 cm (55 x 172½ in); oil on plaster
One of the largest of the Black Paintings in the House of the Deaf
Man, *The Pilgrimage of Saint Isidore,* was in the ground-floor room on
the wall opposite *The Great He-Goat* (p. 51). Considering its unusual
proportions, Goya created a great sense of space within a format
more suited to a shallow frieze design. The snake-like procession
twists and doubles back on itself far into the distance, over the
undulating landscape. The white-robed figures on the farthest hill
seem huddled together for warmth, and have an eerie phosphorescence.

The man's nose is
given definition
by a dab of paint

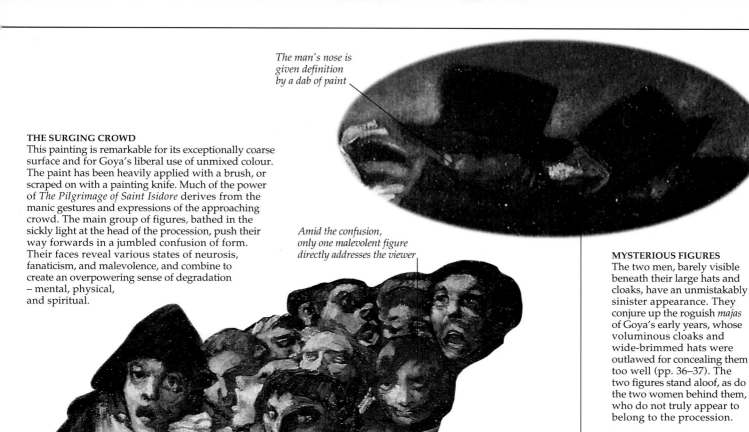

THE SURGING CROWD

This painting is remarkable for its exceptionally coarse
surface and for Goya's liberal use of unmixed colour.
The paint has been heavily applied with a brush, or
scraped on with a painting knife. Much of the power
of *The Pilgrimage of Saint Isidore* derives from the
manic gestures and expressions of the approaching
crowd. The main group of figures, bathed in the
sickly light at the head of the procession, push their
way forwards in a jumbled confusion of form.
Their faces reveal various states of neurosis,
fanaticism, and malevolence, and combine to
create an overpowering sense of degradation
– mental, physical,
and spiritual.

*Amid the confusion,
only one malevolent figure
directly addresses the viewer*

MYSTERIOUS FIGURES

The two men, barely visible
beneath their large hats and
cloaks, have an unmistakably
sinister appearance. They
conjure up the roguish *majas*
of Goya's early years, whose
voluminous cloaks and
wide-brimmed hats were
outlawed for concealing them
too well (pp. 36–37). The
two figures stand aloof, as do
the two women behind them,
who do not truly appear to
belong to the procession.

THE GUITARIST

The grotesque figure leading the procession
recalls Goya's late portrait of the blind
singer Tío Paquete (p. 49). The exaggerated
mannerisms and gaping mouth seem
dislocated and meaningless, hinting at Goya's
own condition of deaf isolation at the time.

The last years in Spain

O<small>N</small> 4 A<small>PRIL</small> 1823, with the support of the King of France, Louis XVIII, and his troops, the Hundred Thousand Sons of St. Louis, Ferdinand VII regained absolute rule of Spain. The liberal leader, General Riego (p. 48), was summarily executed, and Ferdinand embarked upon a persecution of the liberals that was even more ruthless than before. Within three weeks of Ferdinand's return to Madrid, Goya signed over the House of the Deaf Man (pp. 48–49) to his 17-year-old grandson, Mariano, fearing confiscation of his property by the King's agents. By the following January, the official trials and purges of liberal sympathizers, which were to continue for the next ten years, were under way. During the years leading up to this ensuing repressive period known as the Ominous Decade, Goya produced his last great series of etchings, *Los Disparates* (The Follies). The thinly disguised political and social satire of these, and his other graphic works, made Goya the likely target of a reactionary backlash. Fearful for his own safety, he went into hiding.

CRUEL FOLLY
c.1815–24; 24.5 x 35 cm (9½ x 13¾ in); etching and aquatint
The Folly prints belong to Goya's series entitled *Los Disparates*, later published as *The Proverbs*. Seemingly disparate in subject matter, they are characterized by a violently anti-clerical stance. Although this image probably derives from Goya's memory of scenes he had witnessed in the asylum in Saragossa (p. 24), it also symbolizes the treachery of the church towards its flock.

SIMPLETON'S FOLLY
c.1815–24; 24.5 x 35 cm (9½ x 13¾ in); etching and aquatint
Bobalicón is a gigantic fool, whose name was given to this work in the 19th century. He derived his original identity from a Spanish carnival idiot. Just as Goya's *Colossus* can be interpreted as an allegory of war (p. 39), this over-grown fool is symbolic of the primitive beliefs and practices that were encouraged by the Church and exploited by the Inquisition. The lumbering, grinning simpleton of monstrous proportions is Goya's manifestation of the superstitious worship of holy images. The stiff, hooded figure with which the monk entices the simpleton and behind which he hides, evokes one of the papier mâché puppets paraded on feast days. Popular in appeal, it represents the antithesis of enlightened thinking.

FEARFUL FOLLY
c.1815–24; 24.5 x 35 cm
(9½ x 13¾ in); etching and aquatint
This print satirizes superstition, which held
great sway over the Spanish people. The
"giant" here, however, is only a trickster
whose human identity is discernible through
the sleeve of the giant's clothing.

**MAN PICKING FLEAS
FROM A LITTLE DOG**
*1824–25; 9 x 8.5 cm (3½ x
3¼ in); oil on ivory*
While in hiding, in
the winter of 1824–25,
Goya took up the art
of miniature painting.
He described his 40
paintings on ivory as
"more like the brush-
work of Velázquez
than that of Mengs"
(pp. 16–17). Goya's
technique involved
blackening the ivory,
dropping water onto it,
and then improvising
from the arbitrary
highlights it created.

SELF-PORTRAIT
1824; 7 x 8 cm (2¾ x 3 in); pen and sepia ink
Goya did this drawing in his 78th year. By
this time his mistress, Leocadia (pp. 48–49)
was already living in Bordeaux, where
according to the city records of 1823, she
sought asylum for her own political opinions.

MARIA MARTINEZ DE PUGA
1824; 80 x 58.5 cm (31½ x 23 in)
This is one of the last portraits that Goya
painted before he went into exile. Its
wonderful simplicity of composition, and
colour, combine with the subject's relaxed
pose to create one of Goya's most intimate
works. The visible alterations, and rapid
execution of the wall and clothing lend the
painting a very modern feel, reminiscent
of the portraits of the French painter
Edouard Manet (1832– 83). Maria Martínez
de Puga is thought to have been the wife of
Antonio de Puga. It is likely that Goya painted this endearing portrait in gratitude to her
husband, who was responsible for overseeing
the continued payment of Goya's salary as
Court Painter, once Goya had left Madrid.

Exile in France

By THE AUTUMN OF 1824, Goya had settled in Bordeaux, in the south-west of France, with his mistress Leocadia Zorilla, her son Guillermo (who was escaping political persecution), and ten-year-old daughter, Rosario. There they lived in the company of fellow exiles, including Goya's old friend Moratín (pp. 28–29). It was at this late stage in his life, when most artists' active production has ceased, that Goya entered another creative phase. At the age of 79, he mastered a difficult new printing process, lithography (p. 63), and produced a brilliant series of lithographs, *Bulls of Bordeaux*. Three years later, he painted *The Milkmaid of Bordeaux*, which, despite his failing eye-sight and old age, ranks as his last great creation.

VIEW OF BORDEAUX
In 1824, Goya moved into a house at 24 Cours de Tourny, in Bordeaux. He lived here with his "second family", Leocadia Zorilla, and her children.

PORTRAIT OF GAULON
1824–25; 27 x 21 cm (10½ x 8¼ in); lithograph
Goya had taken up lithography when he was still living in Madrid, but without much success. It was not until he met the master printer, Cyprien Gaulon, at his workshop in Bordeaux, that he really made the medium his own. Gaulon produced a hundred copies of the published edition of Goya's four prints, *Bulls of Bordeaux*.

BULLFIGHT PRINTS
This title page (left) and plate (below) are from one of the popular editions of prints on Spanish life produced during Goya's lifetime.

GOYA, THE MATADOR
The matador embodied a national image of hot-blooded Spanish *machismo*. Goya himself claimed to have taken part in a bull-fight as a young man.

THE DIVIDED RING
1825; 30 x 41.5 cm (11¾ x 16¼ in); lithograph
This dynamic image is one of the set of lithographs that Goya produced as the *Bulls of Bordeaux*. Bullfighting was a subject with which he had experimented at great length in Madrid in 1815–16, when he created his extensive series of 33 engravings, *The Art of Bullfighting*, also known as *La Tauromaquia*.

BULLFIGHT TRIPTYCH
1817; 20 x 15 cm (8 x 5¾ in)
Painted before Goya's departure to France, and after his *Art of Bullfighting* series, these paintings demonstrate how Goya continued the same artistic themes into his exile. They depict a selection of bloody dramas, which appear to take place in an open landscape. The passion of bullfighting appealed to Goya, who was an avid huntsman in his youth.

The Milkmaid of Bordeaux

1825–27; 74 x 68 cm (29 x 26½ in)

Goya painted this charming painting when he was 81 years old. It was not a commissioned work, but a purely private enterprise that seems, above all, to be a celebration of beauty, and an affirmation of life. This last brilliant burst prompted his old friend Moratín to write of the artist: "He is very cocksure these days and paints furiously, never wanting to correct anything he paints."

THE CHURN
Goya included the churn in the left-hand corner as a symbol with which to identify his sitter, the milkmaid. She was one of the young country girls who delivered milk to his house in Bordeaux.

INDIVIDUALITY
Goya's brushwork reveals a sublime indifference to the fashion of the day, represented by the slick, fussy style and surface polish of the new First Painter to King Ferdinand VIII, Vicente López (p. 60).

BRUSHWORK
Here, Goya's relaxed, supremely confident handling of paint, despite its apparently crude application, achieves a sensuous, tremulous quality also present in Velázquez' late paintings (p. 34).

Goya dies at eighty

Goya's last palette

IN 1825, GOYA SUFFERED A DEBILITATING illness, from which he never recovered. He was unwell when he made the arduous journey to Madrid in 1826, where Vicente López (1772–1850), who had been First Court Painter since 1815, painted his portrait (bottom left). Goya's eyesight became so poor that he had to work with the aid of a magnifying glass. Despite this, his final two series of drawings and lithographs (below and right) reveal his great energy and tireless preoccupation with human folly. In April 1828, aware of his rapidly deteriorating condition, he wrote to his son Javier: "May God grant that I see you ... and then my happiness will be complete". Goya died on the night of 15 April, in Bordeaux, where he was buried. In 1929, his remains were removed to their final resting place, a tomb in San Antonio de la Florida (pp. 32–33).

OLD MAN ON SWING
1824–28; black chalk
This celebratory image features an old man recklessly indulging in past pleasures. A later reworking of the drawing introduces a mortality theme, in the form of attendant phantoms.

PORTRAIT OF GOYA
Vicente López; 1828;
93 x 75 cm (36½ x 29½ in)
This is one of the few existing painted portraits of Goya. He is reputed to have had a hand in it himself, adding touches of his own and insisting that the fastidious academic painter López stop when Goya considered the portrait finished.

GREAT COLOSSUS ASLEEP
1824–28; black chalk
Here, Goya's *Colossus* appears for the last time, his great head resting on the ground as he sleeps. Tiny figures swarm over him – one waves a flag – but, since he is only sleeping and not dead, their triumph will not last. An allegory of Spain's violent history, this sad image reveals Goya's pessimism regarding his country's future.

I AM STILL LEARNING
1824–25; black chalk

Following the cathartic Black Paintings (pp. 48–55), Goya's last works explored gentler themes (p. 59). He, however, lost none of his cruel wit and sardonic vision of the human condition. He now spent much of his time drawing, returning to old subjects, and recording scenes of Bordeaux and Paris, which he had briefly visited. This drawing is inscribed with the words *Aun aprendo*, "I am still learning", and though not a self-portrait, it clearly represents Goya's indefatigable spirit.

LETTER TO ZAPATER
In this letter to his old friend Martín Zapater Goya complains of ageing before his time. Typical of Goya's consistently childlike sense of humour, he has written the last part of the letter with his finger dipped into the ink.

OLD WOMAN WITH MIRROR
1824–28; 18.5 x 13.5 (7¼ x 5¼ in); black chalk

Goya's portrayals of old age are often interpreted as purely satirical – allegories of vanity or lust, for instance. However, this rather touching drawing of an old woman reveals a certain compassion, and an understanding of the infirmities of old age – heightened, perhaps, by the deterioration of his own health and failing eyesight.

GOYA'S TOMB
This record of Goya's tomb in Bordeaux was painted by his friend, the young artist Antonio Brugada. Goya's body was originally interred in the vault of a distant family relative, Martin Miguel de Goicoechea, and in 1901 removed to Madrid. In 1929, Goya's remains were exhumed once more and moved to a tomb in the Hermitage of San Antonia de la Florida, the site of the artist's last great fresco. Brugada made the first inventory of works after Goya's death in 1828. The purely descriptive, and often misleading, titles that he attributed to Goya's paintings have now become permanent fixtures.

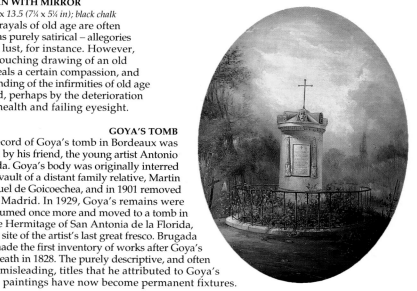

Key biographies

Duchess of Alba A great beauty, she is supposed to have been the love of Goya's life.

Francisco Bayeu (1734-1795) Goya's elder by 12 years, he was also from Saragossa. His career presented a brilliant role model for the young Goya. He assisted Anton Mengs in the decoration of the Royal Palace in Madrid. He also supervised work at the Royal Tapestry Factory. Appointed Painter to the King, he later became Director of the Academy.

Ramón Bayeu (1746-1793) Goya's exact contemporary, who initially received a head start through his brother Francisco's influence. He was ultimately less successful than Goya – happy to imitate his brother's style in his paintings and cartoons.

Joseph I, Bonaparte (1768-1846) The usurper King of Spain (1808-13), he was the eldest brother of Napoleon.

Charles III (1716-88) An "enlightened" King, who reformed Spain's economy and strengthened the Crown's authority over the Church.

Charles IV (1784-1819) An ineffectual ruler, who was dominated by his wife María Luísa and Manuel Godoy. After France's invasion, he abdicated in favour of his son, and then Joseph Bonaparte in 1808.

Ferdinand VII, Bourbon (1783-1833) An ill-fated reactionary monarch. He intrigued against his father Charles III in 1807, and was banished from Madrid. Only king for a brief period after his father's abdication in 1808, he was usurped by the Bonaparte regime. He recovered his throne in 1813 with the help of the British, but refused to accept the liberal Constitution of Cadiz (1812) and initiated a period of counter-revolutionary terror. Obliged to recognize the 1812 Constitution in 1820; three years later he reinstated repressive absolutism.

Corrrado Giaquinto (1703-1765) Working in Naples and Spain, he decorated the new royal palaces. His dark style with flickering light and dramatic figures influenced Goya's early works.

Manuel Godoy (1767-1851) The favourite of the Queen, he was extremely unpopular throughout Spain. Godoy became Prime Minister in 1792. He led Spain into a series of disasters culminating in Napoleon's invasion of 1808.

Vicente López (1772-1850) Goya's successor as First Painter to the King.

José Luzán Trained Goya and the Bayeus in his studio at Saragossa.

Anton Raphael Mengs (1728-1779) Born in Dresden, he came to work in Spain at the invitation of Charles III in 1761. In 1772, he directed young Spanish painters, including Goya, at the Royal Tapestry Factory. His portraits were enormously influential in Spain. His Neo-Classical imagery became Court convention.

María Luisa of Parma The unpopular Queen of Charles IV, who was artistically and politically dominant at the Bourbon court.

Giambattista Tiepolo (1696-1770) One of the greatest Venetian fresco painters. In 1761, Charles III invited him to Madrid to paint the throne room. His frescos were a great influence on Goya and his contemporaries. They were exemplary in their application and brushwork, offering a whole new range of imagery.

Diego Velázquez (1599-1660) Spain's most renowned painter and the ultimate role model for Goya. He was one of the few artists in Spain's history who gained a status comparable to that of the great foreign painters.

Duke of Wellington (1769-1852) Sent by the British Parliament to command various European expeditions, he led the victory of Salamanca in 1812 and finally drove the French out of Spain in 1814.

Martín Zapater Goya's oldest friend from Saragossa. The two men corresponded throughout their lives. Today, the letters provide vital documentation of Goya's life.

Leocadia Zorilla A distant cousin of Goya's, she was his housekeeper and mistress in his old age.

The exterior of Goya's birthplace in Fuendetodos

Goya collections

The following shows the locations of museums and galleries around the world that own five or more works by Francisco Goya.

NORTH AMERICA
Boston Museum of Fine Arts
Cambridge, MA Fogg Art Museum,
Chicago Art Institute of Chicago
Dallas Meadows Museum
New York Frick Collection;
Hispanic Society of America;
Metropolitan Museum of Art

EUROPE
France
Bayonne Musée Bonnat
Paris Musée du Louvre

Germany
Berlin Staatliche Museen Preussischer Kulturbesitz
Hamburg Kunsthalle
Munich Alte Pinakothek

Netherlands
Rotterdam Museum Boymans-van Beuningen

Spain
Madrid Biblioteca Nacional; Calcografía Nacional; Fundación Lázaro Galdiano; Museo del Prado; Palacio Real; Real Academia de Bellas Artes de San Fernando; Real Academia de la Historia; San Antonio de la Florida
Valencia Museo Provincial de Bellas Artes
Saragossa Basilica of Our Lady of the Pillar; Charterhouse of Aula Dei; Museo Provincial de Bellas Artes

Sweden
Stockholm Nationalmuseum

Switzerland
Winterthur Sammlung Oskar Reinhart "Am Römerholz"

UK
London British Museum; National Gallery

Glossary

Aquatint creates a wash effect

Al secco The fresco technique, in which oils were painted directly onto plaster walls.

Aquatint A printing process which produces an effect resembling a wash drawing. A plate is dusted with acid-resistant particles and untreated areas are eaten away by immersion in an acid bath, leaving behind a granular effect.

Baroque Artistic movement originating in Rome during the 17th century, typified by its dynamic movement, emotional display, and use of florid ornament.

Cartoon A full-size drawing made to transfer a design onto a tapestry or painting. Painters at the Royal Tapestry Factory first made small preliminary oil sketches before painting the final cartoon, which would be copied by the weavers, after the King had approved it.

Drypoint An etching technique where the design is scratched straight onto the copper plate with a needle. Due to the raised "burr" (ridges of waste metal created by the incised design), drypoint has a soft, rich, quality.

Etching A printing technique in which a plate is first covered with an acid-resistant ground, on which the artist draws, exposing the surface. When the plate is immersed in acid the drawn areas are bitten away. Ink collects in these lines and is then printed.

Fresco The wall-painting technique in which pigment, mixed with water, is applied to a layer of wet plaster. When dry, the wall and the colours are inseparable.

Ground A preparatory surface of primer or paint applied to the canvas.

Impasto Paint applied in thick, raised strokes.

Lavis An etching technique simulating ink wash on paper.

Lithography A print produced by drawing on a porous stone with lithographic ink or greasy crayon. The stone is wetted and greasy ink is applied, which, due to the antipathy of ink and water, will adhere only to the drawn lines. This impression can then be printed on dampened paper.

Mezzotint A process in which a metal plate is roughened with a rocking tool, creating a burr on the surface. Where light tones are required, the burr is scraped away: where the plate remains rough it will hold the ink and create areas of intense black. A mezzotint produces areas of tone rather than distinct lines.

Neo-Classicism The dominant style in art during the late 18th and early 19th centuries, inspired by the renewed interest in Classical Rome and Greece. Its severity contrasts with the light-hearted, decorative qualities of the Rococo style.

Palette The flat surface on which an artist sets out and mixes paints. Also the range of colours used.

Pentimento A correction showing through the picture surface.

Picture plane The imaginary plane represented by the physical surface of a painting.

Primer A neutral coloured paint used to seal the canvas or surface before paint is applied.

Rococo The style of art that originated in France around 1700, reacting against ornate Baroque. It was characterized by lightness, grace, and the delicate play of surface.

Sfumato A soft, smoky effect, created by colours and tones overlapping and blending, changing imperceptibly from light to dark.

Tempera Paint in which pigment is dissolved in water and mixed with gum or egg white.

Wet-in-wet The application of one colour of paint into or next to another, before the first is dry.

Primer showing through the paint surface

Goya works on show

The following is a list of the museums and galleries that exhibit the paintings by Goya reproduced in this book.

Unless otherwise stated, all works in this book are oil on canvas.

t= top, b= bottom, l= left, r= right, c= centre

Prado= Museo de Prado, Madrid
Real Academia= Real Academia de Bellas Artes de San Fernando, Madrid

p. 8 b: *The Adoration of the Name of God*, Basilica El Pilar, Saragossa.
p. 9 t: *The Circumcision*, Aula Dei, Saragossa; bl: *Virgin of the Pillar*, Museo de Zaragoza; br: *Portrait of a Young Man*, Museo de Zaragoza.
p. 10 l: *The Hunter and his Dog*, Prado; cr: *Dogs in Leash*, Prado.
p. 11 b: *The Picnic*, Prado.
p. 12 tl: *The Amateur Bullfight*, Prado; bl: *The Crockery Vendor*, Prado.
p. 13 cl: Oil Sketch for *The Washerwomen*, Oskar Reinhart Collection "Am Römerholz", Winterthur; br: *The Washerwomen*, Prado.
p. 14–15 *The Parasol*, Prado.
p. 16 bl: *Christ on the Cross*, Prado.
p. 17 r: *St. Bernardine of Siena*, San Francisco El Grande, Madrid; bl: *The Queen of Martyrs*, Basilica El Pilar, Saragossa.

p. 18 cl: *Self-portrait at Easel*, Real Academia.
p. 19 l: *The Marchioness of Pontejos*, National Gallery of Art, Washington.
p. 20 bl: *The Wounded Mason*, Prado; cr: *Winter*, Prado; br: *Summer*, Museo Lázaro Galdiano, Madrid.
p. 21 tl: *Charles IV*, Museo de Bellas Artes, Córdoba; tr: *The Wedding*, Prado; cl: *The Straw Mannikin*, Prado; b: *The Meadow of St. Isidore*, Prado.
p. 22 cr: *Boys playing at Soldiers*, Pollok House, Glasgow Museums; br: *Boys with Mastiffs*, Prado.
p. 23 tl: *The Little Giants*, Prado; r: *Don Manuel Osorio Manrique de Zuñiga*, The Metropolitan Museum of Art, New York.
p. 24 bl: *The Madhouse at Saragossa*, Meadows Museum, Dallas; br: *Sebastián Martinez*, The Metropolitan Museum of Art, New York.
p. 25 tl: *The Shipwreck*, Palacio Real, Madrid; cl: *Portrait of Francesco Bayeu*, Prado.
p. 26 cr: *Marchioness of Solana*, Louvre, Paris; bl : *Duchess of Alba and her Duenna*; br: *Duke of Alba*, Prado.
p. 27 l: *Duchess of Alba*, The Hispanic Society of America, New York; cr: *The Matador Pedro Romero*, Kimbell Art Museum, Fort Worth, Texas.
p. 28 tr: *Self-portrait with Spectacles*,

Museo Camón Aznar, Saragossa; cl: *Portrait of Martín Zapater*, Museo Bellas Artes, Bilbao.
p.29 cr: *Leandro Fernández de Moratin*, Real Academia.
p. 30 cr: *The Family of the Duke of Osuna*, Prado; bl: *The Forcibly Bewitched*, National Gallery, London.
p. 31 tl: *The Spell*, Museo Lázaro Galdiano, Madrid; br: *The Witches Sabbath*, Museo Lázaro Galdiano, Madrid.
p. 32–33 *Miracle of St Anthony of Padua*, San Antonio de la Florida, Madrid.
p. 34 cr: *Manuel Godoy*, Real Academia.
p. 35 tl: *Infante Carlos María Isidro*, Prado; c: *Infante María Josefa*, Prado; tr: *Infante Francisco de Paula Antonio*, Prado; b: *The Family of Charles IV*, Prado.
p. 36 cr: *María Luisa in a Mantilla*, Palacio Real, Madrid; cl: *Naked Maja*, Prado; br: *Clothed Maja*, Prado.
p. 37 l: *Doña Isabel de Porcel*, National Gallery, London.
p. 38 bl: *Making Shot in the Sierra*, Palacio Zarzuela, Madrid; br: *Allegory of the Town of Madrid*, Ayuntamiento, Madrid.
p. 39 tr: *Sheep's Head and Joints*, Louvre, Paris; tl: *Savages Murdering a Woman*, Prado; b: *The Colossus*, Prado.
p. 42 br: *Portrait of the Duke of Wellington*, National Gallery,

London.
p. 43 tl: *Self-portrait*, Real Academia; tr: *Third of May 1808*, Prado; b: *Second of May 1808*, Prado.
p. 44 c: *Procession of Flagellants*; b: *Inquisition Scene*, Real Academia.
p. 45 tl: *Ferdinand VII with Royal Mantle*, Prado; br: *The Burial of the Sardine*, Real Academia.
p. 46 –47 br: *Self-portrait with Dr Arrieta*, The Minneapolis Institute of Arts.
p. 48 tl: *Young Women with a Letter*, Musée Lille; bl: *La Leocadia*, Prado; br: *The Dog*, Prado, .
p. 49 tl: *Duel with Cudgels*, Prado; b: *El Tío Paquete*, Thyssen-Bornemisza Collection, Switzerland.
p. 50 tl: *Two Old Men*, Prado; cr: *Two Old People Eating*, Prado.
pp. 50-51 b: *The Great He-Goat*, Prado.
p. 51 tl: *Saturn*, Prado.
p. 52 cl: *Vision*, Oeffentliche Kunstsammlung, Kunstmuseum, Basel; b: *Asmodea*, Prado.
p. 53 *The Fates*, Prado.
pp. 54-55 b: *The Pilgrimage of St. Isidore*, Prado.
p. 57 tr: *Man Picking Fleas from a Little Dog*, Staatliche Kunstsammlungen, Dresden; br: *Maria Martínez de Puga*, The Frick Collection, New York.
p. 58 bl, bc, br: *Bullfight Triptych*, Museo Camón Aznar, Saragossa.
p. 59 *The Milkmaid of Bordeaux*, Prado.

Index

Acknowledgements

PICTURE CREDITS

Every effort has been made to trace the copyright holders and we apologize in advance for any unintentional omissions. We would be pleased to insert the appropriate acknowledgement in any subsequent edition of this publication.

Key:
t: top b: bottom c: centre l: left r: right

Abbreviations:
AR: Artophot BEP: Basilica El Pilar, Saragossa BL: British Library, London BM: The Trustees of the British Museum, London BN: Bibliothèque Nationale, Paris CNM: Calcografia Nacional, Madrid CNGF: Casa Natal de Goya, Fuendetodos MLG: Museo Lázaro Galdiano, Madrid MM: Museo Municipal, Madrid MET: The Metropolitan Museum of Art MP: © Museo del Prado, Madrid, All Rights Reserved MZ: Museo de Zaragoza NGL: Reproduced by courtesy of The Trustees, The National Gallery, London OR: Oronoz PC: Private Collection PR: Palacio Real, Madrid RA: Real Academia de Bellas Artes de San Fernando, Madrid RFT: Real Fabrica de Tapices, Madrid

Front cover: Clockwise from top left: RA; RA; MP; MM; MP; MP; c: RA **Back cover:** RFT; CNM; MP; RFT; MM; MP; The Parasol (detail), MP (also c, cl); CNM; CNM; CNM; MM; BM

Inside front flap: t: National Gallery of Art, Washington; MP **p1:** RA **p2:** tl: MP; tr: MZ; c: BL; bl, bc: CNM; cr: RA; br: MP **p3:** cl, c: MP; cr: MET, Harris Brisbane Dick Fund, 1935; bl: RFT; bc: MM; br: MLG **p4:** tl, cl, br: MP; tr: CNM; cr, bc: CNGF; bl: RA **p5:** br: MP **p6:** tr, cr, cl, bl, br: CNGF; c: MAS, Barcelona **p7:** tl: MM; tc: Hulton Deutsch Collection; bl: PC/ OR/ AR; r: MZ **p8:** c: BEP/ OR **p9:** tl, bl: Aula Dei, Saragossa/ OR; cr: MM; bl, br: MZ **p10:** l, cr: MP; tr, br: MLG **p11:** tl: MLG; tc, b: MP; tr, cr: MM; cl: MAS, Barcelona **p12:** tl, bl: MP; tr: RFT; br: MAS, Barcelona **p13:** tl, tr: RFT; cl: Oskar Reinhart Collection "Am Römerholz", Winterthur; br: MP **p14:** b: MP **p15:** MP **p16:** tl: MP/ Michael Holford; bl: MP; br: PR/ OR **p17:** tl, tr, cl: CNM; r: San Francisco el Grande, Madrid/ OR; c: MM; bl: BEP/ OR **p18:** tl: BL; cl: RA; cr: Banco de España, Madrid/ OR; bl: PC, Florence/ OR/ AR **p19:** tr: MP; tc: National Gallery of Art, Washington, Andrew W. Mellon Collection **p20:** tl: MLG; tr: Collection Duquesa del Arco, Malaga/ OR/ AR; bl, cr: MP; br: MLG/OR/ AR **p21:** tl: Museo de Bellas Artes, Córdoba/ OR/ AR; tr, cl, b: MP; cr: from Laborde's Voyage Pittoresque et Historique de l'Espagne **p22:** tl, br,: MP; cl: MM; cr: Glasgow Museums: Stirling Maxwell Collection, Pollok House **p23:** tl: MP; r: MET, Jules Bache Collection, 1949 **p24:** tr: RA; tl: BN; bl: Algur H. Meadows Collection, Meadows Museum, Southern Methodist University, Dallas, Texas; br: MET, Rogers Fund, 1906 **p25:** tl: Collection Palacio Real, Madrid/ OR/ AR; tr: PC/ OR/ AR; cl: MP; c: BL; br: RA **p26:** tl: MET, Harris Brisbane Dick Fund, 1935; cr: Louvre, Paris; bl, bc, br: MP **p27:** l: Courtesy of the Hispanic

Society of America, New York; tr:MM; cr: Kimbell Art Museum, Fort Worth, Texas; br: Arxiu MAS **p28:** tr: Museo Camón Aznar, Obra Social de la Caja de Ahorras y Monte de Piedad de Zaragoza Aragón y Rioja, Ibercaja; cl: Museo Bellas Artes, Bilbao/ OR; bl: MLG **p29:** tl, tc, bl, bc, br: CNM; cr: RA **p30:** tl: from Charles Yriarte's Goya, Paris, 1867; cr: MP; br: NGL **p31:** tl, br: MLG; cr: CNM; bl: MP **p32–33:** San Antonio de la Florida/ OR **p34:** tr: MM; bl: Collection Duque de Sueca, Madrid/ OR; c: © Museo del Ejercito, Madrid, All Rights Reserved; cr: RA; br: MP **p35:** MP **p36:** tl: CNM; cl, br: MP; cr: PR/OR **p37:** tl: MLG; tr, l: NGL **p38:** tr, cl: MM; bl: Palacio Zarzuela, Madrid/ OR; br: Ayuntamiento, Madrid/ OR **p39:** tl, b: MP; tr: Louvre,Paris; br: BN **p40:** tl, tr: MM; cr, bl, br: CNM **p41:** tl: MM; tr, cl, cr, bl, br: CNM **p42:** tr, cr: MM bl: BM; br: NGL. **p43:** tl: RA; tr, b: MP **p44:** tl: MP; c, cr, b: RA **p45:** tl: MP; tc, cr: CNM; cl, bl: Museo de Artes y Tradiciones Populares, Madrid/ OR; br: RA **p46–47:** Minneapolis Institute of Arts, Ethel Morrison Van Derlip Fund **p48:** tl: Musée Lille/ AR; tr: from an article by Charles Yriarte in L'Art 1877 Vol II; bl, br: MP **p49:** tl: MP; b: Thyssen-Bornemisza Collection, Switzerland **p50:** tl, cr: MP **p50-51:** b: MP **p51:** MP **p52:** cl: Oeffentliche Kunstsammlung, Kunstmuseum, Basel; b: MP **p53:** c: MP; c, cl: CNM; br: MLG **p54-55:** MP **p56:** tl: MP; cl, br: CNM **p57:** tl: CNM; tr: Kupferstich-Kabinett, Staatliche Kunstsammlungen, Dresden; MP; br: © Frick Collection, New York **p58:** tl: Hulton Deutsch Collection; ctl: Davison Art Center Collection, Middletown; cbl: MM; bl, bc, br: Museo Camón Aznar, Obra Social de la Caja

de Ahorras y Monte de Piedad de Zaragoza Aragón y Rioja. Ibercaja; cr: CNM **p59:** MP **p60:** tl: Courtesy of The Hispanic Society of America, New York; tr: RA; bl: MP; br: Gerstenbergdestr, Berlin/ MAS **p61:** tl: MLG; tr, bl: MP; br: RA **p62:** CNGF **p63:** tl CNM; cr: (detail) Minneapolis Institute of Arts, Ethel Morrison Van Derlip Fund.

Additional Photography

Andy Crawford and his assistant Gary Ombler: All location photography in Spain. Pablo Lines: All photography at the Museo Municipal, Madrid. Stephen Hayward: **p19:** tc. Susannah Price: **p32:** cr. Philippe Sebert: **p26:** cr; **p39:** tr.

Dorling Kindersley would like to thank:
Elvira Villena at the Calcografía Nacional, Madrid, Elisa Picazo Verdejo at the Casa Natal de Goya, Fuendetodos for the images on p6, and Manuel Martín for creating the Grape Harvest on a frame **p13:** tr.

Author's acknowledgements:
I would like to thank Gabriele Sinaldi at the National Gallery for his help and advice, and Emma Shackleton and Jan Green for all their hard work. Special thanks to all those at DK who contributed to this book: Laura Harper, Gwen Edmonds, and Toni Kay; Julia Harris-Voss, Jo Evans, and Job Rabkin for picture research; Anna Kunst for translations; Louise Candlish, Colette Connolly, Sandra Copp, Peter Jones, and Constance Novis for their help; Pip Seymour for technical information; and I would especially like to thank the editor, Helen Castle, and the designer, Liz Sephton, for all their patience and hard work.